WESTERN MYSTICISM

A Guide to the Basic Works

WESTERN MYSTICISM

A Guide to the Basic Works

Compiled by

MARY ANN BOWMAN

Center for Contemplative Studies
Western Michigan University

American Library Association

CHICAGO 1978

Library of Congress Cataloging in Publication Data

Bowman, Mary Ann.
        Western mysticism.

        Includes indexes.
        1. Mysticism—Indexes.   2. Mysticism—Judaism—
Indexes.   I. Title.
Z7819.B68   [BV5082.2]   016.2914'2   78-18311
ISBN 0-8389-0266-9

Printed in the United States of America

CONTENTS

PREFACE

The study of human consciousness and its relationship to our lives and needs has aroused a great deal of interest in today's world. This interest extends into many areas of religion, philosophy, psychology, sociology, and literature. Part of this trend is a renewed interest in mysticism, most of which has been directed toward Oriental mysticism. However, many people are unaware of the rich and vital mystical tradition Western culture has to offer. The purpose of this bibliography is to help create a deeper awareness of Western mysticism.

The term *mysticism* has had many meanings over the centuries. The definition used for this bibliography is that of an intuitive, contemplative approach to fundamental reality, an approach beyond ordinary human conception or reason (but not, in the West, antagonistic to the rational, analytic approach). This approach is often religious but may be secular. The term *Western* is used in the sense of non-Oriental and so includes both Jewish and Eastern Orthodox traditions, which greatly influenced and closely parallel the thought patterns of Western Europe.

This publication is not comprehensive but is rather a selective working bibliography, designed as a guide to the literature for reference librarians in academic, public, and church-related libraries; undergraduate students; and general readers. The appendix, designed for acquisitions librarians, suggests first-purchase choices for libraries wishing to build a basic collection and/or a collection of popular titles in Western mysticism.

Most of the major works listed have been published in many editions, but since the bibliography is concerned with titles rather than editions, only exemplary editions are indicated. Original, rather than reprint, editions are shown. Titles are listed under the main entries used in the *National Union Catalog*. Full author-title and subject indexes detail the contents of the books listed. Each title has been assigned an item number, to which the indexes refer. Many of the contents of collections listed have been analyzed in the indexes, enabling the user to find anthologies in which individual mystical writings appear.

Any process of selection is inevitably somewhat personal and arbitrary, and so readers may find titles and authors that they believe should have been included or omitted. Every effort has been made to include those titles on the subject of mysticism that are readable, clearly presented, and best suited to the undergraduate student and general reader. Chapter 7, Mystical and Contemplative Writings, lists a representative group of authors of various faiths and philosophies, with selection based largely on the overall importance of the individuals' contributions. Materials dealing primarily with the occult—that is, alchemy, astrology, witchcraft, and the like—have not been included.

ACKNOWLEDGMENTS

This bibliography could not have been compiled without the support and guidance of several individuals at Western Michigan University.

Dr. Jean Lowrie, Director of the School of Librarianship, originally involved me in the project. I am especially grateful to her and to Dr. John R. Sommerfeldt, Director of the Center for Contemplative Studies, for their financial and moral support of the bibliography and for their advice and encouragement during its compilation.

The Editorial Advisory Committee has given invaluable guidance. Dr. Guntram Bischoff, Department of Religion; Dr. Edward Callan, Department of English; Dr. E. Rozanne Elder, Editorial Director, Cistercian Publications; Dr. Otto Gründler, Director, The Medieval Institute; Dr. Cornelius Loew, Vice-President for Academic Affairs; and Drs. Lowrie and Sommerfeldt have given generously of their time and expertise.

Thanks are also due to the Reverend Archimandrite Kallistos Ware, Spalding Lecturer in Eastern Orthodox Studies at Oxford University, who graciously took time to read the entire manuscript and to give his suggestions for titles in the Orthodox tradition.

Finally, special thanks go to Father Paschal Phillips of the Trappist-Cistercian Abbey of Our Lady of Guadalupe, who recognized the need for the bibliography, shared his profound knowledge of the field, and encouraged the development of this work.

I. The Philosophy of Mysticism

This chapter includes titles on the theology, meaning, and theory of mysticism.

A-1 Arsen'ev, Nikolai Sergeevich. *Mysticism and the Eastern Church;* introd. by Evelyn Underhill. London: SCM Pr., 1926. 172p.

A Russian scholar on the mystical doctrine of the Eastern Orthodox church.

A-2 Balthasar, Hans Urs von. *Prayer.* New York: Sheed & Ward, 1961. 246p.

A Jesuit priest on the theory of contemplation.

A-3 Baumgardt, David. *Great Western Mystics: Their Lasting Significance.* (Machette Foundation Lectures, no. 4) New York: Columbia Univ. Pr., 1961. xii, 99p.

Scholarly and philosophical approach to the definition and meaning of mysticism.

A-4 Bennett, Charles Andrew Armstrong. *A Philosophical Study of Mysticism, an Essay.* New Haven: Yale Univ. Pr., 1923. 94p.

Concerned with mysticism as a way of life.

A-5 Bergson, Henri Louis. *The Two Sources of Morality and Religion.* New York: Holt, 1935. viii, 308p.

The famous French philosopher on moral obligation and mysticism as dynamic religion.

A-6 Bolle, Kees W. *The Freedom of Man in Myth.* Nashville: Vanderbilt Univ. Pr., 1968. xiv, 199p.

A guide to the reading of myth, showing value of past cultures and relating myth to mysticism.

A-7 Bouyer, Louis. *Introduction to Spirituality.* n.p.: Liturgical Pr., 1961. 321p.

Outlines the various elements of spirituality and discusses aids to contemplation and prayer. By a well-known Roman Catholic scholar.

A-8 Brinton, Howard Haines. *The Religious Philosophy of Quaker-ism.* Wallingford, Pa.: Pendle Hill, 1973. xii, 115p.

The beliefs of Fox, Barclay, and Penn related to the Gospel of Saint John.

A-9 Dupré, Louis K. *The Other Dimension: A Search for the Meaning of Religious Attitudes.* Garden City, N.Y.: Doubleday, 1972. 565p.

A study of religious faith in today's age of secularization.

A-10 Eliade, Mircea. *Myth and Reality.* (World Perspectives, v. 31) New York: Harper, 1963. xiv, 204p.

A famous scholar of the history of religions, on the structure and history of myths.

A-11 ———. *Myths, Dreams and Mysteries.* (Library of Religion and Culture) New York: Harper, 1967. 256p.

Explores the "encounter between contemporary faiths and archaic realities."

A-12 Furse, Margaret Lewis. *Mysticism: Window on a World View.* Nashville: Abingdon, 1977. 220p.

An introduction to mysticism as a pattern of thought and practice.

A-13 Gaynor, Frank, ed. *Dictionary of Mysticism.* New York: Philo-sophical Library, 1953. 208p.

Defines terms used in religious mysticism, occultism, esoteric philosophy, psychical research, and astrology. Includes Oriental religions.

A-14 Ghose, Sisirkumar. *Mystics and Society: A Point of View;* fore-word by Aldous Huxley. London: Asia Publ. House, 1968. xvi, 116p.

Six brief essays on the relationship between the mystic and so-ciety, referring to ancient and modern, Eastern and Western texts. Intended to begin dialogue on the social validity of the mys-tical point of view.

A-15 Goodenough, Erwin Ramsdell. *By Light, Light.* New Haven: Yale Univ. Pr., 1935. xv, 436p.

A scholarly study of the "mystic gospel of Hellenistic Judaism."

A-16 Gregerson, Jon. *The Transfigured Cosmos.* New York: Ungar, 1960. 111p.

Four essays on the mysticism of the Eastern Orthodox church.

A-17 Happold, Frederick Crossfield. *Religious Faith and Twentieth-Century Man.* Baltimore: Penguin, 1966. 184p.

The religious philosophy of mysticism presented as a solution to today's spiritual crisis.

A-18 Harkness, Georgia. *Mysticism: Its Meaning and Message.* Nashville: Abingdon, 1973. 192p.

A survey of mysticism from Saint Augustine to contemporary "neomysticism," by a Methodist author.

A-19 Harper, Ralph. *Human Love, Existential and Mystical.* Baltimore: Johns Hopkins Pr., 1966. 178p.

Studies man's love for the human and for God, with many references to mystical writers.

A-20 Herman, Emily. *The Meaning and Value of Mysticism.* 3d ed. London: J. Clarke, 1922. xvi, 397p.

Examines the nature of mysticism and the contemplative life.

A-21 Heschel, Abraham Joshua. *God in Search of Man.* New York: Farrar, 1955. 437p.

A famous rabbi's interpretation of the historic Jewish faith in contemporary terms, giving insight into the contribution and significance of modern Judaism.

A-22 ———. *Man Is Not Alone.* New York: Farrar, 1951. 305p.

Deals with the problem of knowing God and with the satisfaction of human needs through religious faith, particularly in terms of Judaism.

A-23 Hopkinson, Arthur Wells. *Mysticism, Old and New.* London: Nisbet, 1946. ix, 153p.

A study of the effects of institutions on contemplative religious experience.

A-24 Hügel, Friedrich von. *The Mystical Element of Religion, as Studied in Saint Catherine of Genoa and Her Friends.* London: Dent, 1908. 2v.

A classic work that began the modern trend in Western contemplative studies.

A-25 Inge, William Ralph. *Mysticism in Religion.* London: Hutchinson's Univ. Library, 1947. 178p.

A former dean of Saint Paul's Cathedral, writing on Greek, New Testament, and medieval mysticism.

A-26 James, William. *Varieties of Religious Experience.* New York: Longmans, 1902. xii, 534p.

A classic study by the famous American psychologist, examining religious phenomena from the viewpoint of experimental psychology. Gives the definition of mysticism still used in many contemporary studies.

A-27 Johnson, Pierce. *Dying into Life.* Nashville: Abingdon, 1972. 176p.

The theme of "rising to Christ" through the death of the self related to various individuals' lives, by a Methodist minister.

A-28 Johnson, William Alexander. *The Search for Transcendence.* New York: Harper, 1974. x, 157p.

"A theological analysis of non-theological attempts to define transcendence."

A-29 Jones, Rufus Matthew. *New Studies in Mystical Religion.* New York: Macmillan, 1927. 205p.

Lectures given at Union Theological Seminary by a well-known Quaker scholar. Examines the nature and validity of mystical experience in relation to such topics as the abnormal, asceticism, and religious education.

A-30 Kelsey, Morton T. *Myth, History and Faith.* New York: Paulist, 1974. v, 185p.

A Jungian approach to the "remythologizing of Christianity."

A-31 Knowles, David. *The Nature of Mysticism.* (Twentieth Century Encyclopedia of Catholicism, v. 38, Section 4) New York: Hawthorn, 1966. 140p.

Examines the nature of mystical experience by relating it to the Christian theology of grace. Published in England under the title *What Is Mysticism?*

A-32 Lossky, Vladimir. *The Mystical Theology of the Eastern Church.* London: J. Clarke, 1957. 252p.

A scholarly approach to theology and mysticism in the Eastern tradition.

A-33 Marquette, Jacques de. *Introduction to Comparative Mysticism.* New York: Philosophical Library, 1949. 229p.

Lectures about mystical experience in various world cultures.

A-34 *The Mystic Vision: Papers from the Eranos Yearbooks;* ed. by Joseph Campbell. (Bollingen Series, 30, 6) Princeton, N.J.: Princeton Univ. Pr., 1968. xiii, 487p.

A collection of scholarly papers, including discussions of the mystical in Indian and Chinese mythologies and in the Christian religion.

A-35 Nowell, Robert. *What a Modern Catholic Believes about Mysticism.* Chicago: Thomas More Pr., 1972, 1975. 94p.

An English writer and journalist on the problem of mysticism for the Catholic of today, examining such questions as Is mysticism necessary? and Is mysticism Christian? One of a series of titles presenting the point of view of contemporary Catholicism.

A-36 *Orthodox Spirituality;* by a monk of the Eastern church. New York: Macmillan, 1945. xv, 108p.

"An outline of the Orthodox ascetical and mystical tradition."

A-37 Otto, Rudolf. *The Idea of the Holy.* 2d ed. New York: Oxford Univ. Pr., 1952. xix, 232p.

A classic study of the nonrational factor in religion, by a famous German scholar and theologian.

A-38 Poulain, Augustin François. *The Graces of Interior Prayer: A Treatise on Mystical Theology;* introd. by J. V. Bainvel. St. Louis: Herder, 1950. cxii, 665p.

A classic study intended for the layperson, by a French Jesuit priest of the late 19th century. Comprehensively surveys the nature and problems of prayer.

A-39 Robinson, John Arthur Thompson. *Exploration into God.* (Raymond Fred West Memorial Lectures, 1966) Stanford, Calif.: Stanford Univ. Pr., 1967. vii, 166p.

Examines the Christian vision and the mystical outlook in the light of contemporary theology.

A-40 Scharfstein, Ben-Ami. *Mystical Experience.* Indianapolis: Bobbs-Merrill, 1973. [7] 195p.

A contemporary American philosopher on the examination of mystical experience in terms of rational analysis.

A-41 Scholem, Gershom Gerhard. *Major Trends in Jewish Mysticism.* 3d rev. ed. New York: Schocken, 1954. 460p.

A classic collection of lectures that explores religious thought and experience, analyzing and interpreting the principal features of Jewish mysticism. By a famous scholar.

A-42 Shook, Glen Alfred. *Mysticism, Science and Revelation.* Wilmette, Ill.: Bahá'i Publ. Trust, 1967. x, 145p.

Mysticism in the Bahá'i faith, from the viewpoint of a physicist.

A-43 Spencer, Sidney. *Mysticism in World Religion.* South Brunswick, N.J.: A. S. Barnes, 1966, ©1963. 363p.

A survey of the mystical religions of the entire world.

A-44 Staal, Fritz. *Exploring Mysticism: A Methodological Essay.* Berkeley: Univ. of California Pr., 1975. xix, 230p.

With many references to primary sources, reviews traditional methods by which mysticism has been studied and presents methods that would be more productive. Contends past studies have been flawed by conceptual biases.

A-45 Stace, Walter Terence. *Mysticism and Philosophy.* Philadelphia: Lippincott, 1960. 349p.

A philosophical, analytical study of mystical experience throughout history and among diverse peoples and religions.

A-46 Stiernotte, Alfred P., ed. *Mysticism and the Modern Mind.* New York: Liberal Arts, 1959. 206p.

A collection of symposium papers by eleven philosophers, examining mysticism from a variety of positions.

A-47 Thornton, Martin. *English Spirituality: An Outline of Ascetical Theology.* . . . London: Society for Promoting Christian Knowledge, 1963. xv, 330p.

An introduction to the ascetical theology of the English church.

A-48 Trewothan, Illtyd. *Mysticism and Theology.* London: Chapman, 1975. x, 163p.

An "essay in Christian metaphysics" by an English Roman Catholic monk. Examines religion in terms of Christian belief, revelation, mysticism, and contemporary views on mysticism, finding disagreement with many modern writers and thinkers.

A-49 Underhill, Evelyn. *Mysticism.* New York: Dutton, 1930. xviii, 515p.

A classic study, concerned mainly with Christian mysticism. Examines the nature and development of mystical experience.

A-50 La Vie Spirituelle. *Mystery and Mysticism;* by A. Plé and others. New York: Philosophical Library, 1956. v, 137p.

Six essays by different authors on the meaning of the term "mysticism" in Saint Paul and the early Christian church. First published in French as a special edition of the journal *La Vie Spirituelle.*

A-51 Watkin, Edward Ingram. *The Philosophy of Mysticism.* London: Grant Richards, 1919. 412p.

A classic study of the mystic, mystical experience, and the metaphysics of mysticism, by a Roman Catholic scholar.

A-52 Whitson, Robley Edward. *Mysticism and Ecumenism.* New York: Sheed & Ward, 1966. xv, 209p.

A theological and comparative study, including selections from Christian and non-Christian mystical writings.

A-53 Zaehner, Robert Charles. *Concordant Discord: The Interdependence of Faiths.* New York: Oxford Univ. Pr., 1970. vii, 464p.

Lectures analyzing the mystical traditions of Christianity and several Oriental religions and relating them to the mysticism of Saint Francis de Sales and Teilhard de Chardin.

A-54 ———. *Mysticism, Sacred and Profane.* London: Oxford Univ. Pr., 1957. 256p.

Comparison between religious and naturalistic concepts of mystical experience.

2. The history of Mysticism

This chapter includes titles that approach the study of mysticism through the lives and works of mystical individuals. Additional historical titles appear in chapter 7, Mystical and Contemplative Writings, under the names of the individuals discussed.

B-1   Bancroft, Anne. *Twentieth Century Mystics and Sages*. Chicago: Regnery, 1976. 344p.

Surveys the lives and works of many contemporary figures, from Aldous Huxley to Mother Teresa of Calcutta. Includes photographs of many of the subjects.

B-2   Bigg, Charles. *The Christian Platonists of Alexandria*. Oxford: Clarendon, 1886. 304p.

A series of lectures on Philo, Clement, and Origen.

B-3   Bolshakoff, Sergius. *Russian Mystics;* introd. by Thomas Merton. (Cistercian Studies Series, 26) Kalamazoo, Mich.: Cistercian Publications, 1977. xxx, 303p.

An introduction to the lives, spirituality, and writings of the great Russian mystics.

B-4   Bouyer, Louis. *The Spirituality of the New Testament and the Fathers*. (History of Christian Spirituality, v. 1) New York: Desclee, 1963. xix, 541p.

A detailed history covering the period from Christianity's earliest days to the time of Saint Augustine.

B-5   Bridges, Leonard Hal. *American Mysticism*. New York: Harper, 1970. xi, 208p.

Examines early psychological experiments, mystics from a variety of faiths, and experiences with psychedelic drugs, concentrating on the period from 1900 to the present.

B-6   Brinton, Howard Haines. *Friends for 300 Years.* New York: Harper, 1952. 239p.

The history and beliefs of the Society of Friends, by a prominent Quaker author.

B-7   Bullett, Gerald William. *The English Mystics.* London: Joseph, 1950. 239p.

Gives the medieval English background and discusses several mystical individuals, from George Fox to William Wordsworth.

B-8   Butler, Edward Cuthbert. *Western Mysticism.* 2d ed. with afterthoughts. London: Constable, 1927. xci, 352p.

A classic study on the teachings of Augustine, Gregory, and Bernard about contemplation and the contemplative life. By the abbot of an English Benedictine monastery.

B-9   Cheney, Sheldon. *Men Who Have Walked with God.* New York: Knopf, 1945. xiv, 395p.

The "story of mysticism" told through the lives of several mystics, including two Oriental figures.

B-10   Clark, James Midgley. *The Great German Mystics: Eckhard, Tauler, and Suso.* Oxford: Blackwell, 1949. vii, 121p.

Studies the lives and works of three prominent German mystics.

B-11   Coleman, Thomas William. *English Mystics of the Fourteenth Century.* London: Epworth, 1938. 176p.

Describes the historical background and discusses five mystical figures of the period.

B-12   Curle, Adam. *Mystics and Militants.* New York: Barnes & Noble, 1972. ix, 121p.

A study relating mysticism to social action.

B-13   Fairweather, William. *Among the Mystics.* Edinburgh: T. & T. Clark, 1936. xvi, 145p.

Describes the rise of mysticism in both East and West and surveys post-Reformation Christian mysticism.

B-14   Gebhart, Emile. *Mystics and Heretics in Italy at the End of the Middle Ages.* London: Allen & Unwin, 1922. 283p.

A popularly written attempt to put into proper perspective some leading figures of medieval Italy. Considered a standard study of the inner history of the period.

B-15   Godwin, George Stanley. *The Great Mystics.* London: Watts, 1945. v, 106p.

The lives and works of eleven mystics of various historical periods.

B-16   Graef, Hilda C. *The Light and the Rainbow.* Westminster, Md.: Newman, 1959. 414p.

A detailed study of the history of Christian spirituality and the contemplative life, from the Old Testament to modern times.

B-17 ———. *Mystics of Our Times.* Garden City, N.Y.: Hanover House, 1962. 240p.

Essays on the lives of ten modern contemplatives, several of whom were active in public affairs.

B-18 ———. *The Story of Mysticism.* Garden City, N.Y.: Doubleday, 1965. 286p.

Briefly examines non-Christian mysticism and surveys mysticism from New Testament times to the late Middle Ages.

B-19 Heschel, Abraham Joshua. *A Passion for Truth.* New York: Farrar, 1973. xv, 336p.

The story of two founders of Hasidism, a movement of the 18th and 19th centuries that strove for a mystical revival within Judaism. Shows their similarities with and differences from each other and Søren Kierkegaard.

B-20 Hodgson, Geraldine Emma. *English Mystics.* Milwaukee: Morehouse, 1922. xi, 387p.

English mysticism from its beginnings to the 17th century.

B-21 Hodgson, Phyllis. *Three Fourteenth-Century Mystics.* Rev. ed. London: Longmans, 1967. 47p.

Three short studies on Richard Rolle, the author of *The Cloud of Unknowing,* and Walter Hilton.

B-22 Inge, William Ralph. *Christian Mysticism.* 8th ed. London: Methuen, 1948. xvi, 379p.

A classic study of the history and development of Christian forms of mysticism.

B-23 ———. *Studies of English Mystics.* London: J. Murray, 1906. 239p.

Examines six English mystics, including Browning and Wordsworth.

B-24 Jones, Rufus Matthew. *The Flowering of Mysticism.* New York: Macmillan, 1939. 270p.

History of Friends of God movement of the 14th century.

B-25 ———. *Spiritual Reformers in the 16th and 17th Centuries.* London: Macmillan, 1914. li, 362p.

A spiritual history of the period, showing the mystical roots in the background from which Quakerism developed.

B-26 ———. *Studies in Mystical Religion.* London: Macmillan, 1909. xxxviii, 518p.

Classic studies on mysticism from the time of primitive Christianity to the English Commonwealth period.

B-27   Katsaros, Thomas, and Kaplan, Nathaniel. *The Western Mystical Tradition*. New Haven, Conn.: College & University Pr., 1969. 324p.

An intellectual history of Western civilization, from early Greek beginnings to the Renaissance.

B-28   Knowles, David. *The English Mystical Tradition*. New York: Harper, 1961. 197p.

A survey of English mysticism, including its Catholic theology and historical period. By a Roman Catholic priest.

B-29   Knox, Ronald Arbuthnott. *Enthusiasm*. New York: Oxford Univ. Pr., 1950. viii, 622p.

A thorough survey of the history of religion, emphasizing the 17th and 18th centuries.

B-30   Kovalevsky, Pierre. *Saint Sergius and Russian Spirituality*. Crestwood, N.Y.: St. Vladimir's Seminary Pr., 1976. 190p.

The life, work, and spiritual heritage of a 14th-century saint.

B-31   Leclercq, Jean. *The Love of Learning and the Desire for God*. New York: Fordham Univ. Pr., 1961. 415p.

"A study of monastic culture."

B-32   ———; Vandenbroucke, François; and Bouyer, Louis. *The Spirituality of the Middle Ages*. (History of Christian Spirituality, v. 2) New York: Desclee, 1968. x, 602p.

A detailed and scholarly survey of the period.

B-33   Lee, Umphrey. *Historical Backgrounds of Early Methodist Enthusiasm*. (Studies in History, Economics and Public Law) New York: Columbia Univ. Pr., 1931. 176p.

Describes the background of enthusiasm in Western Christendom up to the 17th century and English enthusiasm at the time of the Methodist movement.

B-34   Lossky, Vladimir. *The Vision of God*. Clayton, Wis.: American Orthodox Pr., 1964. 168p.

Surveys the Eastern Orthodox tradition up to the 14th century.

B-35   Maloney, George A. *The Cosmic Christ*. New York: Sheed & Ward, 1968. 309p.

Mystical theology of Christ "from Paul to Teilhard."

B-36   Meyendorff, Jean. *Saint Gregory Palamas and Orthodox Spirituality*. Crestwood, N.Y.: St. Vladimir's Seminary Pr., 1974. 184p.

Examines the spiritual tradition of Eastern monks; Saint Gregory Palamas; and Hesychasm, a spiritual movement that began with a community of Greek monks on Mount Athos in the 14th century who wanted a revival of mysticism.

B-37 Ozment, Steven E. *Mysticism and Dissent*. New Haven: Yale Univ. Pr., 1973. xii, 270p.

Mystical theology described as a dissent theology and related to social protest of the 16th century.

B-38 Peers, Edgar Allison. *Studies of the Spanish Mystics*. New York: Macmillan, 1951. 2v.

Studies of mystics of the Renaissance era. Includes section on individuals not otherwise noted in English texts.

B-39 Pepler, Conrad. *The English Religious Heritage*. St. Louis: Herder, 1958. 444p.

Medieval English mystics examined by a Roman Catholic priest through such themes as conversion, the progress of Christian life, and the way of wisdom.

B-40 Petersson, Robert Torsten. *The Art of Ecstasy*. New York: Atheneum, 1970. xv, 183p.

Relates the works of Saint Teresa of Avila to later Teresan works, Bernini's Cornaro Chapel in Rome, and the sacred poetry of Richard Crashaw.

B-41 Scholem, Gershom Gerhard. *Kabbalah*. (Library of Jewish Knowledge) New York: Quadrangle/N.Y. Times Book Co., 1974. 492p.

The historical development, basic ideas, and influences of the Kabbalah, the esoteric mystic lore of Judaism that was handed down as a secret doctrine to the initiated. Includes topics and personalities, with biographical sketches. By a professor of Jewish mysticism at Hebrew University in Jerusalem.

B-42 Seesholtz, Anna Groh. *Friends of God*. New York: AMS Pr., 1970. viii, 247p.

A scholarly study of this 14th-century movement, presenting the social and economic background of the period, religious importance of the movement, and some of its most notable figures.

B-43 Smith, Margaret. *An Introduction to the History of Mysticism*. New York: Macmillan, 1930. vi, 121p.

Surveys mysticism from Hebrew and New Testament times to the medieval period.

B-44 ———. *Studies in Early Mysticism in the Near and Middle East*. New York: Macmillan, 1931. x, 276p.

A study of asceticism and monasticism in early Christianity and Sufism.

B-45 *The Spirituality of Western Christendom;* ed. by E. Rozanne Elder. (Cistercian Studies Series, 30) Kalamazoo, Mich.: Cistercian Publications, 1976. xxxv, 217p.

A collection by various scholars, surveying individuals and movements within Christianity, from Augustine to Calvin.

B-46 Squire, Aelred. *Asking the Fathers.* New York: Morehouse-Barlow, 1973. iii, 248p.

An introduction to many of the great Christian masters, by a Roman Catholic priest.

B-47 Stace, Walter Terence. *The Teachings of the Mystics.* New York: New American Library, 1960. 240p.

A survey of world mysticism, with selections by and analysis and interpretation of many mystical authors of East and West.

B-48 Underhill, Evelyn. *Mystics of the Church.* New York: Schocken, 1964. 259p.

The lives, philosophies, theologies, and influences of the important Christian mystics, from Biblical times to the end of the 17th century.

B-49 Walsh, James, ed. *Pre-Reformation English Spirituality.* New York: Fordham Univ. Pr., 1965. xiii, 287p.

A collection of scholarly essays by various authors on many English religious figures, most well known as mystics.

B-50 ———. *Spirituality through the Centuries.* New York: Kenedy, 1964. ix, 342p.

A collection of scholarly essays by various authors on ascetics and mystics of the Western church.

B-51 Weiner, Herbert. *9½ Mystics: The Kabbala Today.* New York: Holt, 1969. ix, 310p.

A "personal, popular" approach to the Jewish mystical tradition as it exists today.

B-52 Wiesel, Eliezer. *Souls on Fire.* New York: Random, 1972. 268p.

Portraits and legends of Hasidic masters, leaders of the movement of Hasidism. (For explanation of Hasidism, see B-19.) By a well-known Jewish writer.

B-53 Younghusband, Francis Edward. *Modern Mystics.* London: J. Murray, 1935. 315p.

Discusses Hindu and Moslem mystics, Saint Thérèse of Lisieux, and some less-known mystics of the early 20th century.

3. ᴄʜᴇ ᴘʀᴀᴄᴛɪᴄᴇ ᴏꜰ ᴍʏꜱᴛɪᴄɪꜱᴍ

This chapter includes titles on meditation, prayer, and contemplation.

C-1 Bloom, Anthony. *Living Prayer*. Springfield, Ill.: Templegate, 1966. viii, 125p.

Examines the place of prayer in the daily concerns of modern Christians. By the archbishop of the Russian Orthodox Patriarchal Church in Britain.

C-2 Boylan, Eugene. *The Difficulties in Mental Prayer*. Westminster, Md.: Newman, 1966. xiv, 127p.

A Cistercian monk on the nature and technique of the different stages of prayer, from the point of view of the individual. Considered a classic of modern spirituality.

C-3 Brooke, Avery. *Doorway to Meditation, in Words and Pictures*. Drawings by Robert Pinart. Norton, Conn.: Vineyard Books, 1973. 111p.

A narrative about meditation in the Judeo-Christian tradition. Text hand lettered by the illustrator and accompanied by line drawings.

C-4 ———. *How to Meditate without Leaving the World*. Norton, Conn.: Vineyard Books, 1975. 96p.

A step-by-step description of ways to learn and teach meditation.

C-5 *Contemplative Community;* ed. by Basil Pennington. (Cistercian Studies Series, 21) Washington: Cistercian Publications, 1972. 366p.

A collection of papers by various scholars on the monastic tradition and the liturgy, theology, sociology, anthropology, and psychology of contemplative community.

C-6   Doherty, Catherine DeHueck. *Poustinia.* Notre Dame, Ind.: Ave
Maria Pr., 1975. 216p.

Conferences for Eastern Orthodox solitaries. Written by the
founder of Madonna House, a spiritual center in Ontario.

C-7   Evdokimoff, Paul. *The Struggle with God.* Glen Rock, N.J.: Paulist, 1966. vi, 218p.

Writings on the spiritual life from the Russian Orthodox approach.

C-8   Fox, Matthew. *On Becoming a Musical, Mystical Bear: Spirituality, American Style.* New York: Harper, 1972. xvi, 156p.

A discussion of prayer as the center of individual spirituality,
and a call to the experience of mysticism and prophecy.

C-9   Grou, Jean Nicholas. *How to Pray: Nine Chapters on Prayer from
the School of Jesus Christ.* Nashville: Upper Room, 1973. 96p.

A simple guide to prayer by a French Jesuit of the 18th
century.

C-10   Happold, Frederick Crossfield. *The Journey Inwards.* London:
Darton, Longman & Todd, 1968. 142p.

"A simple introduction to the practice of contemplative meditation by normal people."

C-11   ———. *Prayer and Meditation.* Baltimore: Penguin, 1971. 381p.

A study of the nature and practice of prayer and meditation,
along with a collection of prayers, devotions, and meditations.

C-12   Heschel, Abraham Joshua. *Man's Quest for God: Studies in
Prayer and Symbolism.* New York: Scribner, 1954. 151p.

A famous Jewish scholar on modern man's need for prayer.

C-13   Hinson, E. Glenn. *A Serious Call to a Contemplative Life Style.*
Philadelphia: Westminster, 1974. 125p.

A Baptist professor of church history on the problem of devel-
oping devotional life in a technological society.

C-14   Ignatii, Bishop of Caucasus and Chernomor'e. *On the Prayer of
Jesus: From the Ascetic Essays of Bishop Ignatius Brianchaninov.*
London: John Watkins, 1965. 114p.

A 19th-century Eastern Orthodox bishop on Hesychastic
prayer. (See B-36 for explanation of Hesychasm.)

C-15   Jacobs, Louis. *Hasidic Prayer.* (Littman Library of Jewish Civilization) New York: Schocken, 1972. ix, 195p.

A systematic study of methods of prayer, including contemplative and ecstatic prayer, drawing parallels with practices of other
religious traditions. By a rabbi. (*See* B-19 for explanation of
Hasidism.)

C-16   *Jesus in Christian Devotion and Contemplation;* by Irénée Noye and others. St. Meinrad, Ind.: Abbey Pr., 1974. xvi, 116p.

A collection of articles by five Roman Catholic priests and nuns on the history of devotion and contemplation.

C-17   Kelsey, Morton. *The Other Side of Silence.* New York: Paulist, 1975. 314p.

A guide to Christian meditation, emphasizing beginning steps from the standpoint of Jungian psychology.

C-18   LeSaux, Henri. *Prayer,* by Abhishiktananda. Philadelphia: Westminster, 1967. 81p.

A guidebook for Indian Christians by a French Benedictine priest who lives as a holy man in the Himalayas.

C-19   LeShan, Lawrence. *How to Meditate.* Boston: Little, 1974. 210p.

A thorough guide to meditation by a practicing psychotherapist.

C-20   Louf, André. *Teach Us to Pray.* Chicago: Franciscan Herald, ©1975. 112p.

A French Trappist monk on "learning a little about God." Presents the teachings of the early and medieval masters on prayer in terms of the personal and the applied.

C-21   McNamara, William. *The Human Adventure.* Garden City, N.Y.: Doubleday, 1974. 190p.

An appeal for more immediate contact and communication with God, addressed to the layman. Relates personal experiences and offers new language and examples for the insights of classical mysticism. By a hermit monk of the Discalced Carmelite order.

C-22   Maloney, George A. *The Breath of the Mystic.* Denville, N.J.: Dimension Books, 1974. 204p.

A study of mystical prayer based on teachings of Eastern Orthodox mystics and of major contemporary theologians.

C-23   ———. *Inward Stillness.* Denville, N.J.: Dimension Books, 1976. 236p.

An introductory guide to silent prayer and meditation in the light of modern psychology.

C-24   Nouwen, Henri J. *Reaching Out.* Garden City, N.Y.: Doubleday, 1975. 120p.

A Dutch priest and psychologist on three stages of spiritual life: from loneliness to solitude, hostility to hospitality, illusion to prayer. Examines the demands and rewards of the Christian life.

C-25   O'Flaherty, Vincent M. *Let's Take a Trip: A Guide to Contemplation.* Staten Island, N.Y.: Alba House, 1971. 177p.

A handbook from which a "novice could learn without a master," based on the contemplative writings of Ignatius of Loyola.

C-26   Oliver, Fay Conlee. *Christian Growth through Meditation.* Valley Forge, Pa.: Judson Pr., 1976. 124p.

An approach to meditation "beyond transcendental meditation."

C-27   Paulsell, William O. *Taste and See.* Nashville: Upper Room, 1976. 88p.

"A personal guide to the spiritual life" by a Disciples of Christ minister and professor of religion. Gives instruction to deepen and nurture the personal relationship with God, focusing on silence, meditation, prayer, and devotional procedures.

C-28   Pearce, Joseph. *The Crack in the Cosmic Egg.* New York: Julian, 1971. xv, 207p.

A personal, contemporary approach which contends that a new world view must be evolved.

C-29   Pennington, Basil. *Daily We Touch Him.* Garden City, N.Y.: Doubleday, 1977. 115p.

"Practical religious experiences."

C-30   Raguin, Yves. *How to Pray Today.* (Religious Experience Series, v.4) St. Meinrad, Ind.: Abbey Pr., 1974. 60p.

Spiritual reflections and a guidebook to meditation and contemplation, by a European Jesuit who lived in China for many years.

C-31   ———. *Paths to Contemplation.* (Religious Experience Series, v.6) St. Meinrad, Ind.: Abbey Pr., 1974. ix, 154p.

A guide to the spiritual life, presented in a manner derived from traditional Chinese pedagogy.

C-32   Rahner, Karl. *Encounters with Silence.* Westminster, Md.: Newman, 1960. 87p.

Meditations about different aspects of everyday living, presented as dialogues with God. By a well-known Catholic theologian and professor at the University of Innsbruck.

C-33   Sjögren, Per-Olof. *The Jesus Prayer.* Philadelphia: Fortress, 1975. 96p.

A guide to the use of the Eastern Orthodox prayer, by the dean of Gothenburg Cathedral, Sweden.

C-34   Slade, Herbert Edwin William. *Exploration into Contemplative Prayer.* New York: Paulist, 1975. 221p.

A practical guidebook by an Anglican priest, emphasizing methodology rather than theology. Includes exercises to stimulate the contemplative experience and blends Eastern and Western traditions.

C-35 Smith, Bradford. *Meditation: The Inward Art*. Philadelphia: Lippincott, 1963. 224p.

Many aspects of meditation, including Oriental, group, and Quaker meditation, presented by a Quaker author.

C-36 Sontag, Frederick. *Love beyond Pain*. New York: Paulist, 1977. 137p.

"Mysticism within Christianity" examined as a quest for love.

C-37 Underhill, Evelyn. *Practical Mysticism*. New York: Dutton, 1914. xv, 163p.

A classic on the practice of the mystical life.

C-38 Vogel, Arthur. *The Power of His Resurrection*. New York: Seabury, 1976. 106p.

Emphasizes the mystical element latent in traditional devotion to the resurrected Jesus.

C-39 Voillaume, René. *The Need for Contemplation*. Denville, N.J.: Dimension Books, 1972. 79p.

An introduction to contemplation in the Roman Catholic church of today, notable for its brevity and simplicity. Discusses the love of Jesus and prayer and is partly devotional in nature.

C-40 Ware, Kallistos. *The Power of the Name: The Jesus Prayer in Orthodox Spirituality*. (Fairacres Publications, no.43) Oxford: SLG Pr., 1974. 25p.

An eminent Oxford scholar and monk of the Eastern Orthodox tradition examines the importance of Hesychastic prayer for the spirituality of the Orthodox church. (See B-36 for explanation of Hesychasm.)

C-41 Whelan, Joseph P. *Benjamin: Essays in Prayer*. New York: Paulist, 1972. 122p.

Almost free-verse expression of prayer as contemplation, illustrated with drawings. By a Jesuit.

4. the experience of mysticism

This chapter lists titles on the psychology of mysticism, religious consciousness, altered states of consciousness, and the use of drugs to alter consciousness.

D-1 Blum, Richard H. *Utopiates*. Chicago: Aldine, 1966. xvi, 303p.

A collection of papers by various scientists on the use of LSD, including discussion of the relationship between psychedelic drug use and religious belief. A publication of the Institute for the Study of Human Problems, Stanford University.

D-2 Braden, William. *The Private Sea: LSD and the Search for God*. New York: Quadrangle, 1967. 255p.

Relates the LSD movement to the new theology of John Robinson and Thomas Altizer and to humanistic psychology. By a journalist who studies philosophy and theology.

D-3 Bucke, Richard Maurice. *Cosmic Consciousness*. Rev. ed. New York: Dutton, 1946. xviii, 384p.

A classic early study in the theory of higher consciousness.

D-4 Clark, Walter Houston. *Chemical Ecstasy*. New York: Sheed & Ward, 1969. ix, 179p.

A study of psychedelic drug use in relation to religion, by a psychologist of religion.

D-5 Greeley, Andrew M. *Ecstasy: A Way of Knowing*. Englewood Cliffs, N.J.: Prentice-Hall, 1974. viii, 150p.

A popular approach to the psychology of ecstasy and mysticism, by a Roman Catholic priest, sociologist, and author.

D-6 Grof, Stanislav. *Realms of the Human Unconscious*. New York: Viking, 1975. xxiii, 257p.

Observations from LSD research on psychodynamic, perinatal, and transpersonal experiences.

D-7 Huxley, Aldous Leonard. *The Doors of Perception.* New York: Harper, 1970. 79p.

Visionary experiences during the use of mescaline.

D-8 Johnson, Raynor Carey. *The Imprisoned Splendour.* New York: Harper, 1954. 424p.

Examines the significance of data from the fields of natural science, psychical research, and mystical experience.

D-9 ———. *Watcher on the Hills.* New York: Harper, 1959. 188p.

Studies mystical experiences of ordinary people and relates them to stages expounded by the great mystics.

D-10 Johnston, William. *Silent Music.* New York: Harper, 1974. 190p.

"The science of meditation" examined by a Jesuit priest who teaches at a Tokyo university.

D-11 Laski, Marghanita. *Ecstasy: A Study of Some Secular and Religious Experiences.* Bloomington: Indiana Univ. Pr., 1962. xii, 544p.

A study based on questionnaire answers from people who had experienced mystical states.

D-12 LeShan, Lawrence. *The Medium, the Mystic, and the Physicist.* New York: Viking, 1974. xxix, 299p.

The approaches to reality of the clairvoyant, the mystic, and the physicist, examined by a practicing psychotherapist.

D-13 Leuba, James Henry. *The Psychology of Religious Mysticism.* Rev. ed. (International Library of Psychology, Philosophy, and Scientific Method) New York: Harcourt, 1929. 336p.

A classic early study by a professor of psychology, with reference to both Yoga and Christian mysticism.

D-14 Marechal, Joseph. *Studies in the Psychology of the Mystics.* London: Burns, Oates & Washbourne, 1927. vii, 344p.

Another classic in the psychology of mysticism, by a Jesuit priest.

D-15 Maslow, Abraham Harold. *Religions, Values, and Peak-Experiences.* Columbus: Ohio State Univ. Pr., 1964. xx, 123p.

Peak-experiences and the need for spiritual expression discussed in terms of humanistic psychology.

D-16 Milner, Dennis, and Smart, Edward. *The Loom of Creation.* New York: Harper, 1976. 319p.

Experimental evidence for forces of creation described by mystics, presented by two English scientific/technical researchers.

D-17 Mishlove, Jeffrey. *The Roots of Consciousness.* New York: Random, 1975. xxxiv, 341p.

A detailed survey of historical and scientific approaches to the study of consciousness, including those of many famous mystics. Has illustrations and an extensive bibliography.

D-18 Naranjo, Claudio, and Ornstein, Robert. *On the Psychology of Meditation.* New York: Viking, 1971. 248p.

Naranjo on the spirit and techniques of meditation, and Ornstein on the implications of meditation techniques for modern psychology.

D-19 Ornstein, Robert Evans, ed. *The Nature of Human Consciousness.* New York: Viking, 1974, ©1973. xiii, 514p.

A collection of readings by various authors with a scientific approach to the study of human consciousness.

D-20 ————. *The Psychology of Consciousness.* New York: Viking, 1972. xii, 274p.

A discussion of consciousness through the concept of a bi-functional brain, by a research psychologist and teacher.

D-21 Pratt, James Bissett. *The Religious Consciousness.* New York: Macmillan, 1920. viii, 488p.

A classic study with several chapters on mystical experience.

D-22 *Psychiatry and Mysticism,* ed. by Stanley R. Dean. Chicago: Nelson-Hall, 1975. xxii, 424p.

A collection of twenty-six papers, mostly by psychiatrists, but intended for both professional and general readers. From three panel-symposia presented at meetings of the American Psychiatric Association to help bridge the gap between medical science and psychical research.

D-23 Tart, Charles T., ed. *Altered States of Consciousness.* New York: Wiley, 1969. 575p.

A collection of articles by various authors on such topics as hypnosis, meditation, psychedelic drugs, and dream consciousness. Edited by a psychologist.

D-24 ————. *Transpersonal Psychologies.* New York: Harper, 1975. 502p.

A collection of writings by Tart and others on the scientific interpretation of mystical experience and its psychological significance.

D-25 Van Dusen, Wilson Miles. *The Natural Depth in Man.* New York: Harper, 1972. 197p.

A psychologist's phenomenological study of fantasy, prayer, dreams, hypnagogic states, hallucination, and mystical experience. Includes appendix on Emanuel Swedenborg.

D-26 Walker, Kenneth Macfarlane. *The Mystic Mind.* New York: Emerson, 1965. 176p.

Discusses consciousness as related to mystical experience. 1st ed. published under the title *The Conscious Mind.*

D-27 White, John Warren, ed. *The Highest State of Consciousness.* Garden City, N.Y.: Doubleday, Anchor Books, 1972. xvii, 484p.

A collection of thirty-three articles on a wide range of topics related to the mystical consciousness. Authors include Aldous Huxley, Alan Watts, R. D. Laing, Abraham Maslow, and other scholars, scientists, and writers.

D-28 Zaehner, Robert Charles. *Zen, Drugs, and Mysticism.* New York: Pantheon, 1973, ©1972. 223p.

A critique of contemporary mysticism; contends that drug experiences contrast greatly with true mystical experiences. British ed. published under the title *Drugs, Mysticism, and Make-Believe.*

5. ORIENTAL MYSTICISM
IN WESTERN CONTEXTS

E-1 Déchanet, Jean Marie. *Christian Yoga.* New York: Harper, 1960. 196p.

Yoga theory, exercises, and techniques presented in terms of Christian faith and Western customs, by a French Benedictine.

E-2 Dumoulin, Heinrich. *Christianity Meets Buddhism.* (Religious Encounters: East and West) LaSalle, Ill.: Open Court, 1974. 206p.

An examination of Buddhism and Christianity in dialogue, from a theological point of view.

E-3 Graham, Aelred. *Contemplative Christianity.* New York: Harcourt, 1965. x, 131p.

An exploration of the integration of Oriental methods of contemplation into Western Christianity.

E-4 ———. *Zen Catholicism: A Suggestion.* New York: Harcourt, 1963. 228p.

Evaluates Zen from a Roman Catholic point of view, including supplements on Yoga, monasticism, and Thomas Aquinas.

E-5 Griffiths, Bede. *Return to the Center.* Springfield, Ill.: Templegate, 1976. 146p.

Restatement of Christian theology by a Christian monk living in a Hindu-style monastic community.

E-6 ———. *Vedanta and Christian Faith.* Los Angeles: Dawn Horse Pr., 1973. x, 89p.

An examination of the importance of contemplation in creating a unified world culture.

E-7 Johnston, William. *Christian Zen.* New York: Harper, 1971. viii, 109p.

An Irish Jesuit who lived many years in Japan presents insights into Oriental methods of contemplative prayer gained from

Buddhist friends. Draws parallels between the Zen experience and the Christian mystical tradition.

E-8   ———. *The Still Point: Reflections on Zen and Christian Mysticism.* New York: Fordham Univ. Pr., 1970. xiii, 193p.

Discusses Zen enlightenment, Christian mystical experience, and the intuitive approach to reality.

E-9   Lassalle, Hugo. *Zen Meditation for Christians.* (Religious Encounters: East and West) LaSalle, Ill.: Open Court, 1974. 175p.

A presentation of Zen for Christians, comparing the two mystical traditions.

E-10   Otto, Rudolf. *Mysticism, East and West.* New York: Macmillan, 1960. 282p.

A comparative analysis by a prominent German theologian and scholar.

E-11   Raguin, Yves. *The Depth of God.* (Religious Experience Series, v.10) St. Meinrad, Ind.: Abbey Pr., 1975. xi, 145p.

Christianity expressed in the light of the Chinese humanism of Confucianism, Taoism, and Buddhism. By a European Jesuit expert in Chinese language and culture.

E-12   Suzuki, Daisetz Teitaro. *Mysticism, Christian and Buddhist.* (World Perspectives, v.12) New York: Harper, 1957. 214p.

A collection of studies by a famous Buddhist scholar, relating the teachings of Meister Eckhart to those of Zen and Shin.

E-13   Watts, Alan Wilson. *This Is It, and Other Essays on Zen and Spiritual Experience.* New York: Pantheon, 1960. 158p.

Essays on the nature of spiritual or mystical experience and its relation to ordinary material life.

E-14   Wu, Ching-Hsiung. *Chinese Humanism and Christian Spirituality: Essays of John C. H. Wu.* (Asian Philosophical Studies, no.2) Jamaica, N.Y.: St. John's Univ. Pr., 1965. ix, 227p.

A Roman Catholic convert on such topics as Confucius, Saint Thérèse, Chinese ethics, and Christian faith.

6. mystical expression in literature

This chapter includes critical works on mysticism in literature. Mystical works of literature are listed in chapter 7, Mystical and Contemplative Writings.

F-1 *Anagogic Qualities of Literature;* ed. by Joseph P. Strelka. (Yearbook of Comparative Criticism, v.4) University Park: Pennsylvania State Univ. Pr., 1971. vii, 335p.

A collection of essays by various contributors on the relationships between literature and mystic or esoteric traditions, from Christian mysticism to Zen Buddhism.

F-2 Andreach, Robert J. *Studies in Structure.* New York: Fordham Univ. Pr., 1964. ix, 177p.

A study of the treatment of the stages of the spiritual life in Hopkins, Joyce, Eliot, and Hart Crane.

F-3 Bremond, Henri. *Prayer and Poetry.* London: Burns, Oates & Washbourne, 1927. vii, 200p.

A classic study of mysticism in literature, concentrating mostly on the French tradition. Examines the poetical theory of classicism, romanticism, and mysticism.

F-4 Brockington, Alfred Allen. *Mysticism and Poetry on a Basis of Experience.* London: Chapman & Hall, 1934. xv, 224p.

Concepts of vision and the mystical outlook, with many references to and examples from poets, mystics, and writers on mysticism.

F-5 Broers, Bernarda Conradina. *Mysticism in the Neo-Romanticists.* Amsterdam: H. J. Paris, 1923. viii, 233p.

A study of several poets, including Rossetti, Patmore, Francis Thompson, Swinburne, and the Pre-Raphaelites.

F-6   Collins, Joseph Burns. *Christian Mysticism in the Elizabethan Age*. Baltimore: Johns Hopkins Pr., 1940. xiv, 251p.

    A thorough study of mystical literature of foreign origin, and of Christian mysticism in general and in native English writers.

F-7   Doughty, William Lamplough. *Studies in Religious Poetry of the Seventeenth Century*. London: Epworth, 1946. xiv, 199p.

    Discusses six devotional poets of the period.

F-8   Durr, R. A. *Poetic Vision and the Psychedelic Experience*. Syracuse, N.Y.: Syracuse Univ. Pr., 1970. 275p.

    Attempts to show a relationship between psychedelic experiences and the creative in literature and art, citing many comparisons between writings of mystical poets and novelists and reports of drug experiences.

F-9   Grant, Patrick. *The Transformation of Sin*. Amherst: Univ. of Massachusetts Pr., 1974. xiii, 240p.

    Examines the relationship between the religion and the poetry of four Anglican devotional poets.

F-10   Hirst, Désirée. *Hidden Riches*. New York: Barnes & Noble, 1964. xv, 348p.

    A study of symbolism from the Renaissance to William Blake.

F-11   Husain, Itrat. *The Mystical Element in the Metaphysical Poets of the Seventeenth Century*. Edinburgh: Oliver & Boyd, 1948. 351p.

    Relates the personal spiritual experiences of six poets to their works.

F-12   Maritain, Jacques, and Maritain, Raissa. *The Situation of Poetry*. New York: Philosophical Library, 1955. 85p.

    The French Thomist philosopher and his wife, a poet, in four essays on the relationship between poetry, mysticism, magic, and knowledge.

F-13   Martz, Louis Lohr. *The Paradise Within*. New Haven: Yale Univ. Pr., 1964. xix, 217p.

    Examines the style, organization, and meaning of literary works of Henry Vaughan and Thomas Traherne, and of Milton's *Paradise Lost* and *Paradise Regained,* from the standpoint of the Augustinian concept of interior illumination.

F-14   ———. *Poetry of Meditation*. (Yale Studies in English, v.125) New Haven: Yale Univ. Pr., 1954. xv, 375p.

    Suggests that the metaphysical poets were drawn together by resemblances resulting from the common practice of certain methods of religious meditation. A study of the contribution of the meditative art to verse.

F-15 Osmond, Percy Herbert. *The Mystical Poets of the English Church*. New York: Macmillan, 1919. xi, 436p.

Commentary on excerpts from the poets, from Spenser to Evelyn Underhill.

F-16 Spurgeon, Caroline Frances Eleanor. *Mysticism in English Literature*. New York: Putnam, 1913. vii, 168p.

The classic study of mysticism in English literature, examining the "philosophical type of mysticism which concerns itself with questions of ultimate reality." Divides the mystics into four categories: love and beauty; nature; philosophical; and devotional and religious.

F-17 Thompson, Elbert Nevius Sebring. *Mysticism in Seventeenth Century English Literature*. Chapel Hill: n.p., 1921. 63p.

A detailed, scholarly survey of the period; contends that much of the finest literature of the 17th century was written with mystical insight. Attributes this insight to a "mystical strain in the Anglican character."

F-18 Watkin, Edward Ingram. *Poets and Mystics*. London: Sheed & Ward, 1953. ix, 318p.

Essays by a Roman Catholic scholar on poetry, mysticism, and religion.

F-19 White, Helen Constance. *The Metaphysical Poets: A Study in Religious Experience*. New York: Macmillan, 1936. ix, 444p.

A study of the 17th century and of the lives and works of five poets of the period.

F-20 Wilson, Colin. *Poetry and Mysticism*. San Francisco: City Lights Books, 1970. 79p.

Poetic inspiration and mystical consciousness presented as the way to an evolutionary renewal of the human spirit.

F-21 Wright, Luella Margaret. *The Literary Life of the Early Friends, 1650–1725*. New York: Columbia Univ. Pr., 1932. xiv, 309p.

A thorough study of all the forms of literary expression used by the early Quakers.

7. MYSTICAL AND CONTEMPLATIVE WRITINGS

This chapter lists works by and about individual mystics. Representative mystical works are cited for each person listed. In cases where no separately published representative text exists—as, for example, with some of the poet-mystics—a collected edition of the writer's works has been listed. Works listed about the mystics are those that, at least in part, describe the mystical aspect of the individuals' lives and works.

Collections

G-1 Colledge, Eric, ed. *The Mediaeval Mystics of England.* New York: Scribner, 1961. 309p.
     Writings of seven important mystics of the period.

G-2 ————, ed. and tr. *Mediaeval Netherlands Religious Literature.* New York: London House & Maxwell, 1965. 226p.
     Includes several authors not otherwise available in English.

G-3 *Early Fathers from the Philokalia;* sel. and tr. by E. Kadloubovsky and G. E. H. Palmer. London: Faber, 1954. 421p.
     Writings of seven church fathers of the Eastern Orthodox tradition, from the *Philokalia,* the standard collection of Orthodox contemplative writings.

G-4 Eliade, Mircea. *Man and the Sacred.* New York: Harper, 1974. 173p.
     An anthology of ancient religious texts, not including Judaistic or Christian writings.

G-5   Fedotov, Georgii Petrovich, ed. *A Treasury of Russian Spirituality*. New York: Sheed & Ward, 1950. 501p.

Writings of nine figures; each selection preceded by an introduction about its author. Prefaced with a historical overview.

G-6   Fremantle, Anne (Jackson), ed. *The Protestant Mystics*. Boston: Little, 1964. xi, 396p.

Brief selections from more than sixty Protestants, with the term *mystic* broadly defined.

G-7   Gardner, Edmund Garratt, ed. *The Cell of Self-Knowledge.* New York: Suffield, 1910. xxvii, 134p.

Seven early English mystical treatises.

G-8   Happold, Frederick Crossfield. *Mysticism: A Study and an Anthology*. Rev. ed. Baltimore: Penguin, 1970. 407p.

Includes thirty selections, some from Eastern mystics, and precedes each selection with a short introductory essay.

G-9   Hunter, Irene Louise, comp. *American Mystical Verse: An Anthology*. New York: Appleton, 1925. xxiii, 308p.

Includes such writers as Emerson, Longfellow, Whittier, and Dickinson, along with lesser-known authors.

G-10   Huxley, Aldous Leonard. *The Perennial Philosophy*. New York: Harper, 1945. xi, 312p.

Many selections from Eastern and Western mystics, arranged under various headings and embedded in Huxley's interpretation and commentary.

G-11   Jaegher, Paul de, ed. *An Anthology of Mysticism*. Westminster, Md.: Newman, 1950. viii, 281p.

Mystical writings of twenty-two authors, including several less-known Roman Catholic mystics. Has an essay by the editor on "How and Why the Mystics Should Be Read."

G-12   Kepler, Thomas Samuel, ed. *The Fellowship of the Saints*. New York: Abingdon-Cokesbury, 1948. 800p.

Christian devotional literature from the patristic period to the 20th century, including 137 authors, many of them not usually anthologized.

G-13   Khariton, comp. *The Art of Prayer: An Orthodox Anthology;* comp. by Igumen Chariton of Valamo. London: Faber, 1966. 287p.

Monastic authors of the Eastern Orthodox tradition from the 4th to the 20th century, with most from the 19th century.

G-14   Martz, Louis Lohr, ed. *The Meditative Poem: An Anthology of Seventeenth-Century Verse*. New York: New York Univ. Pr., 1963. xxxii, 566p.

Poems by twelve famous 17th-century English poets.

G-15 Newman, Louis Israel, ed. *Hasidic Anthology.* New York: Schocken, 1963. xc, 720p.

Tales and teachings of the Hasidim arranged under more than 200 topical headings. (See B-19 for explanation of Hasidism.)

G-16 O'Brien, Elmer. *Varieties of Mystic Experience.* New York: Holt, 1964. x, 321p.

An anthology and interpretation of more than twenty mystics, many of them from the medieval period. Also includes chapters on Hesychasm, Sufism, Quietism, and Oriental mysticism.

G-17 *The Oxford Book of English Mystical Verse.* Chosen by D. H. S. Nicholson and A. H. E. Lee. Oxford: Clarendon Pr., 1917. xv, 644p.

Verse by such poets as Blake and Crashaw and such mystics as Evelyn Underhill and Arthur E. Waite.

G-18 Peers, Edgar Allison, ed. *The Mystics of Spain.* (Ethical and Religious Classics of the East and West, no. 5) London: Allen & Unwin, 1951. 130p.

Short excerpts from fifteen mystical authors, with a general survey giving the background to their works and personalities.

G-19 Petry, Ray C., ed. *Late Mediaeval Mysticism.* (Library of Christian Classics, v.13) Philadelphia: Westminster, 1957. 424p.

Writings from fifteen mystics of the period, with brief biographical and bibliographical notes preceding most selections.

G-20 Pond, Kathleen, ed. and tr. *The Spirit of the Spanish Mystics.* New York: Kenedy, 1958. 170p.

"An anthology of Spanish religious prose from the 15th to the 17th century."

G-21 Reinhold, Hans Ansgar, ed. *The Soul Afire: Revelations of the Mystics.* New York: Pantheon, 1944. xxiii, 413p.

Many brief selections of writings from various periods and schools of thought, arranged under thematic headings.

G-22 West, Jessamyn, ed. *The Quaker Reader.* New York: Viking, 1962. 522p.

Writings of most of the prominent Quakers of both past and present, along with observations from others, such as Carlyle and Voltaire, about Quakers. Includes a chronology of Quaker history.

G-23 *Writings from the Philokalia on Prayer of the Heart;* sel. and tr. by E. Kadloubovsky and G. E. H. Palmer. London: Faber, 1957. 420p.

Writings of the Eastern church fathers on the Hesychastic method of prayer. (See B-36 for explanation of Hesychasm.)

Ancient, 33–600

Anthony, Saint, *see* Antonius the Great, Saint

ANTONIUS the Great, Saint, 251–356
Known as the founder of Christian monasticism. Lived as a hermit for thirty-five years. Important because his way of life influenced many later writers.

ABOUT ANTONIUS:

H-1 Athanasius, Saint. *The Life of Saint Anthony.* (Ancient Christian Writers, v.10) Westminster, Md.: Newman, 1950. 154p.

Augustine, Saint, *see* Augustinus, Aurelius, Saint

AUGUSTINUS, AURELIUS, Saint, 354–430
Experienced a mystical conversion to Christianity and became an important church leader and bishop of Hippo in North Africa. An influential figure in the evolution of mystical thought.

H-2 *Basic Writings of Saint Augustine.* New York: Random, 1948. 2v.
Especially "On the Morals of the Catholic Church."

H-3 *The Confessions;* tr. by Vernon J. Bourke. (Fathers of the Church, a new tr., v.21) New York: Fathers of the Church, 1953. xxxii, 481p.

ABOUT AUGUSTINUS:

H-4 Brown, Peter Robert Lamont. *Augustine of Hippo: A Biography.* Berkeley: Univ. of California Pr., 1967. 463p.

H-5 Butler, Edward Cuthbert. *Western Mysticism: The Teaching of Augustine, Gregory and Bernard on Contemplation and the Contemplative Life.* London: Constable, 1927. xci, 352p.

H-6 Guardini, Romano. *The Conversion of Augustine.* Westminster, Md.: Newman, 1960. 258p.

H-7 *Saint Augustine;* by M. C. D'Arcy and others. New York: Meridian, 1959. 367p.

Basil, Saint, *see* Basilius, Saint

BASILIUS, Saint, the Great, c.330–379
One of the early church fathers who lived a monastic life for a time and is known as the founder of Eastern monastic institutions.

H-8 *Letters;* tr. by Sister Agnes Clare Way, with notes by Roy J. Deferrari. (Fathers of the Church, a new tr., v.13, 28) New York: Fathers of the Church, 1951–55. 2v.

ABOUT BASILIUS:

H-9 Murphy, Margaret Gertrude. *Saint Basil and Monasticism.* (Catholic Univ. of America. Patristic Studies, v.xxv) Washington: Catholic Univ. of America, 1930. xix, 112p.

Cassian, John, *see* Cassianus, Joannes

CASSIANUS, JOANNES, c.360–c.435
Monk and theologian who founded monastery and convent at Marseilles. Promoted monasticism in Western Europe.

H-10 "Conferences of Cassian," in *Western Asceticism,* ed. by Owen Chadwick. Philadelphia: Westminster, 1958, p.190–289.

ABOUT CASSIANUS:

H-11 Chadwick, Owen. *John Cassian: A Study in Primitive Monasticism.* 2d ed. Cambridge: Cambridge Univ. Pr., 1968. viii, 171p.

Climacus, John, *see* Joannes Climacus

DESERT FATHERS
The first Christian hermits, who settled in the deserts of Egypt and Palestine in the 4th and 5th centuries.

H-12 Apophthegmata Patrum. *The Sayings of the Desert Fathers;* tr. by Benedicta Ward. (Cistercian Studies Series, no.59) Kalamazoo, Mich.: Cistercian Publications, 1975. xviii, 228p.

H-13 Verba Seniorum. *The Wisdom of the Desert;* tr. by Thomas Merton. Norfolk, Conn.: New Directions, 1961, ©1960. ix, 81p.

H-14 Vitae Patrum. *The Desert Fathers;* tr. by Helen Jane Waddell. Ann Arbor: Univ. of Michigan Pr., 1957. 209p.

DIONYSIUS AREOPAGITA, PSEUDO
Unknown Syrian writer of the late 5th century who claimed to be Dionysius of Areopagite, a disciple of Saint Paul. Very influential in development of Western mystical thought.

H-15 *The Divine Names and the Mystical Theology;* tr. by C. E. Rolt. (Translations of Christian Literature, Series 1: Greek Texts) New York: Macmillan, 1920. viii, 223p.

ABOUT DIONYSIUS:

H-16 Rutledge, Denys. *Cosmic Theology: The Ecclesiastical Hierarchy of Pseudo-Denys, an Introduction.* Staten Island, N.Y.: Alba House, 1965, ©1964, xii, 212p.

Dionysius the Pseudo-Areopagite, *see* Dionysius Areopagita, Pseudo

EVAGRIUS PONTICUS, 4th C.
   An influential Greek monk who synthesized the teachings of the Desert Fathers with Greek thought.

H-17 *The Praktikos. Chapters on Prayer;* tr., introd., and notes by John Eudes Bamberger. (Cistercian Studies Series, 4) Spencer, Mass.: Cistercian Publications, 1970, ©1972. xciv, 96p.

GREGORIUS, Saint, Bishop of Nyssa, c.330–394
   One of the fathers of the Eastern church.

H-18 *From Glory to Glory: Texts from Gregory of Nyssa's Mystical Writings;* sel. and introd. by Jean Daniélou. New York: Scribner, 1961. xiv, 298p.

H-19 *The Lord's Prayer. The Beatitudes;* tr. and annotations by Hilda Graef. (Ancient Christian Writers, 18) Westminster, Md.: Newman, 1954. v, 210p.

ABOUT GREGORIUS:

H-20 Cherniss, Harold Fredrik. *The Platonism of Gregory of Nyssa.* Berkeley: Univ. of California Pr., 1930. 92p.

GREGORIUS NAZIANZENUS, Saint, 330–390
   A patriarch of Constantinople.

H-21 "Select Orations and Select Letters," in *Select Library of Nicene and Post-Nicene Fathers of the Christian Church.* 2d Series, v.7. New York: Christian Literature, 1894, p.185–498.

ABOUT GREGORIUS NAZIANZENUS:

H-22 Ruether, Rosemary Radford. *Gregory of Nazianzus: Rhetor and Philosopher.* New York: Oxford Univ. Pr., 1969. viii, 184p.

Gregory of Nazianzus, *see* Gregorius Nazianzenus

Gregory of Nyssa, *see* Gregorius, Saint, Bishop of Nyssa

IGNATIUS, Saint, Bishop of Antioch, 1st C.
   One of the early Christian martyrs.

H-23 *Epistles of St. Ignatius, Bishop of Antioch;* tr. by J. H. Strawley. London: Society for Promoting Christian Knowledge, 1935. vii, 132p.

JOANNES CLIMACUS, Saint, 6th C.
   A hermit monk of the Eastern church.
H-24 *The Ladder of Divine Ascent;* tr. by Archimandrite Lazarus Moore, introd. by M. Heppel. (Classics of the Contemplative Life) New York: Harper, 1959. 270p.

John Cassian, *see* Cassianus, Joannes

John Climacus, *see* Joannes Climacus

MACARIUS, Saint, the Elder, of Egypt, 4th C.
   Lived in the Egyptian desert in extreme austerity for sixty years.
H-25 *Fifty Spiritual Homilies;* tr. by A. J. Mason. (Translations of Christian Literature, Series 1, Greek Texts) New York: Macmillan, 1921. li, 316p.

Origen, *see* Origenes

ORIGENES, c.185–c.253
   One of the great Christian thinkers and scholars of the Alexandrian school and a pupil of Clement of Alexandria.
H-26 *On First Principles;* introd. by Henri de Lubac. New York: Harper, 1966. lxiv, 342p.
H-27 *Prayer. Exhortation to Martyrdom;* tr. and annotated by John J. O'Meara. (Ancient Christian Writers, v. 19) Westminster, Md.: Newman, 1954. vii, 253p.
H-28 *Selections from the Commentaries and Homilies of Origen;* tr. by R. B. Tollinton. New York: Macmillan, 1929. lviii, 272p.
H-29 *Treatise on Prayer;* tr. and notes with account of the practice and doctrine of prayer from New Testament times to Origen by Eric George Jay. London: Society for Promoting Christian Knowledge, 1954. x, 237p.
   ABOUT ORIGENES:
H-30 Daniélou, Jean. *Origen.* New York: Sheed & Ward, 1955. 343p.
H-31 Faye, Eugène de. *Origen and His Work.* London: Allen & Unwin, 1926. 192p.

PACHOMIUS, Saint, c.292–348

Founder in Egypt of the first monasteries as we know them. By the time of his death directed several thousand men in nine cenobitic (monastic) centers and outlined a rule for them that influenced Saint Benedict.

ABOUT PACHOMIUS:

H-32 *Pachomius: The Life of Pachomius: Vita Prima Graeca;* tr. by Apostolos N. Athanassakis, introd. by Birger A. Pearson. (Early Christian Literature Series, 2) (Texts and Translations of the Society of Biblical Literature, 7) Missoula, Mont.: Scholars Press for the Society of Biblical Literature, 1976. xi, 201p.

PAUL, Saint, apostle, d. c.64

The New Testament author.

ABOUT PAUL:

H-33 Schweitzer, Albert. *The Mysticism of Paul the Apostle.* New York: Holt, 1931. xv, 411p.

H-34 Wikenhauser, Alfred. *Pauline Mysticism.* New York: Herder, 1960. 255p.

Philo, *see* Philo Judaeus

PHILO JUDAEUS, 20 B.C.–40 A.D.

Influential philosopher of Alexandria who synthesized the main principles of Neoplatonism with Judaism.

H-35 *About the Contemplative Life;* ed. by F. C. Conybeare. Oxford: Clarendon Pr., 1895. xvi, 403p.

ABOUT PHILO JUDAEUS:

H-36 Goodenough, Erwin Ramsdell. *An Introduction to Philo Judaeus.* 2d ed. rev. New York: Barnes & Noble, 1963. 167p.

PLOTINUS, c.205–c.270

An influential non-Christian teacher who studied in Alexandria and then established a school in Rome, where he taught the principles of Neoplatonism.

H-37 *The Enneads;* tr. by Stephen McKenna, rev. by B. S. Page, introd. by Paul Henry. New York: Pantheon, 1957. li, 635p.

H-38 *The Philosophy of Plotinus: Representative Books from the Enneads;* sel., tr., and introd. by Joseph Katz. New York: Appleton, 1950. 158p.

ABOUT PLOTINUS:

H-39 Bréhier, Emile. *The Philosophy of Plotinus.* Chicago: Univ. of Chicago Pr., 1958. 204p.

H-40   Rist, John M. *Plotinus: The Road to Reality.* Cambridge: Cambridge Univ. Pr., 1967. vii, 280p.

Polycarp, Saint, *see* Polycarpus, Saint

POLYCARPUS, Saint, Bishop of Smyrna, d. 156
   Convert of Saint John, martyr, and last of the subapostolic fathers.
   ABOUT POLYCARPUS:
H-41   "Martyrdom of Polycarp," in *The Didache, The Epistle of Barnabas, The Epistles and the Martyrdom of Polycarp, The Fragments of Papias, The Epistle to Diognetus;* tr. and annot. by James A. Kleist. Westminster, Md.: Newman, 1948, p.83–102.

Pseudo-Dionysius, *see* Dionysius Areopagita, Pseudo

Early Medieval, 601–1200

Aelred of Rievaulx, *see* Ethelred, Saint

ANSELM, Saint, 1033–1109
   A native of Italy who became a monk and archbishop of Canterbury.
I-1   *The Prayers and Meditations of Saint Anselm;* tr., introd., and notes by Sister Benedicta Ward. Harmondsworth, England: Penguin, 1973. 287p.
   ABOUT ANSELM:
I-2   Southern, Richard William. *Saint Anselm and His Biographer: A Study of Monastic Life and Thought, 1059–c.1130.* Cambridge: Cambridge Univ. Pr., 1963. xvi, 389p.

BERNARD DE CLAIRVAUX, Saint, 1091–1153
   Founder of the abbey at Clairvaux, France, and one of the Latin fathers of the church. A powerful and influential church leader. Considered the greatest mystic of the period.
I-3   *Five Books on Consideration: Advice to a Pope;* tr. by John D. Anderson and Elizabeth T. Kennan. (Cistercian Fathers Series, no.37) Kalamazoo, Mich.: Cistercian Publications, 1976. 222p.

I-4 *The Letters of St. Bernard of Clairvaux;* tr. by Bruno Scott James. London: Burns & Oates, 1953. xx, 530p.

I-5 *On the Song of Songs;* tr. by Killian Walsh. (Cistercian Fathers Series, no.4, 7) Washington: Cistercian Publications, 1971–76. 2v.

I-6 *Treatises.* (Cistercian Fathers Series, no.1, 13, 19) Washington: Cistercian Publications, 1970–76. 3v.

ABOUT BERNARD

I-7 *Bernard of Clairvaux: Studies Presented to Dom Jean Leclercq.* (Cistercian Studies Series, no.23) Washington: Cistercian Publications, 1973. xii, 264p.

I-8 Gilson, Etienne. *The Mystical Theology of Saint Bernard.* New York: Sheed & Ward, 1955. ix, 266p.

I-9 James, Bruno S. *Saint Bernard of Clairvaux: An Essay in Biography.* London: Hodder & Stoughton, 1957. 192p.

I-10 Leclercq, Jean. *Bernard of Clairvaux and the Cistercian Spirit.* (Cistercian Studies Series, no.16) Kalamazoo, Mich.: Cistercian Publications, 1976. 178p.

Damian, Peter, *see* Pietro Damiani

ETHELRED, Saint, 1109–1166
The abbot of the monastery at Rievaulx in Yorkshire. One of the first to understand the role of personal friendship in religious experience.

I-11 *Spiritual Friendship;* tr. by Mary Eugenia Laker, introd. by Douglas Roby. (Cistercian Fathers Series, no.5) Washington: Cistercian Publications, 1974. 144p.

I-12 *Treatises. The Pastoral Prayer;* introd. by David Knowles. (Cistercian Fathers Series no.2) (Works of Aelred of Rievaulx, v.1) Spencer, Mass.: Cistercian Publications, 1971. xiii, 128p.

ABOUT ETHELRED:

I-13 Hallier, Amedee. *The Monastic Theology of Aelred of Rievaulx: An Experiential Theology;* special introd. by Thomas Merton. (Cistercian Fathers Series, no.2) Washington: Cistercian Publications, 1969. xxxi, 178p.

I-14 Squire, Aelred. *Aelred of Rievaulx: A Study.* London: Society for Promoting Christian Knowledge, 1969. xii, 177p.

Guiges II, *see* Guigo II

Guiges du Chastel, *see* Guigo I

Guigo I, 1083–1137
Carthusian monk who reinvigorated the order and put its basic rules in writing. Also known as a spiritual writer and considered a master of the mystical life.

I-15 *Meditations of Guigo, Prior of the Charterhouse;* tr. and introd. by John J. Jolin. (Medieval Philosophical Texts in Translation, no.6) Milwaukee: Marquette Univ. Pr., 1951. 84p.

Guigo II, d. c.1188
Carthusian monk and spiritual writer.

I-16 *The Scale of the Cloister: A Treatise on the Art of Mental Prayer;* tr. by Bruno S. James. London: Burns & Oates, 1937. xi, 40p.

Guillaume de Saint-Thierry, 1085–1148
A Benedictine abbot whose friendship with Bernard of Clairvaux influenced his decision to become a Cistercian.

I-17 *The Enigma of Faith;* tr., introd., and notes by John D. Anderson. (Cistercian Fathers Series, no.9) (Works of William of St. Thierry, v.3) Washington: Cistercian Publications, 1974. vii, 122p.

I-18 *Exposition on the Song of Songs;* tr. by Mother Columba Hart, introd. by J. M. Déchanet. (Cistercian Fathers Series, no.6) (Works of William of St. Thierry, v.2) Spencer, Mass.: Cistercian Publications, 1970. xlviii, 171p.

I-19 *The Golden Epistle;* tr. by Theodore Berkeley, introd. by J. M. Déchanet. (Cistercian Fathers Series, no.12) (Works of William of St. Thierry, v.4) Spencer, Mass.: Cistercian Publications, 1971. xxxiii, 117p.

I-20 *On Contemplating God. Prayers. Meditations;* tr. by Sister Penelope, introds. by Jacques Hourlier and J. M. Déchanet. (Cistercian Fathers Series, no.3) (Works of William of St. Thierry, v.1) Spencer, Mass.: Cistercian Publications, 1971. 199p.

ABOUT GUILLAUME:
I-21 Déchanet, Jean Marie. *William of St. Thierry: The Man and His Work.* (Cistercian Studies Series, no.10) Spencer, Mass.: Cistercian Publications, 1972. x, 172p.

Hugh of Saint Victor, *see* Hugo of Saint Victor

Hugo of Saint Victor, 1096–1141
A mystical theologian who spent most of his adult life at the Abbey of Saint Victor, Paris.

I-22   *Selected Spiritual Writings;* introd. by Aelred Squire. (Classics of the Contemplative Life) New York: Harper, 1962. 196p.

ISAAC, Bishop of Nineveh, 7th C.
   A monk of the monastery at Mosul who retired to the Egyptian desert.

I-23   *Mystic Treatises by Isaac of Nineveh;* tr. by A. J. Wensinck. Amsterdam: Koninklijke Akademie van Wetenschappen, 1923. lvi, 400p.

MAXIMUS, Confessor, Saint, c.580–662
   Monk and abbot of Chrysopolis who was a prolific writer on theological, ascetical, and mystical subjects.

I-24   *The Ascetic Life. The Four Centuries on Charity;* tr. and annot. by Polycarp Sherwood. (Ancient Christian Writers, v.21) Westminster, Md.: Newman, 1955, viii, 284p.

ABOUT MAXIMUS:

I-25   Thunberg, Lars. *Microcosm and Mediator: The Theological Anthropology of Maximus the Confessor.* Lund: C. W. K. Gleerup, 1965. xii, 500p.

Peter Damian, *see* Pietro Damiani

PIETRO DAMIANI, Saint, c.1007–1072
   Italian-born reformer who became bishop of Ostia and a doctor of the church.

I-26   *Selected Writings on the Spiritual Life;* tr. and introd. by Patricia McNulty. (Classics of the Contemplative Life) New York: Harper, 1959. 187p.

ABOUT PIETRO DAMIANI:

I-27   Blum, Owen J. *St. Peter Damian: His Teaching on the Spiritual Life.* (Catholic Univ. of America. Studies in Medieval History, n.s., v.10) Washington: Catholic Univ. of America, 1947. viii, 224p.

RICHARD OF SAINT VICTOR, d. 1173
   A Scotsman and scholar of the Abbey of Saint Victor, Paris.

I-28   *Selected Writings on Contemplation;* tr., introd., and notes by Clare Kirchberger. (Classics of the Contemplative Life) New York: Harper, 1957. 269p.

Saint Thierry, Guillaume de, *see* Guillaume de Saint-Thierry

Symeon Neotheologus, 11th C.
A Byzantine monk, better known as Saint Simeon, the New Theologian, who left many writings.

I-29   *Hymns of Divine Love;* tr. by G. A. Maloney. Denville, N.J.: Dimension Books, 1975. 296p.

ABOUT SYMEON:

I-30   Maloney, George A. *The Mystic of Fire and Light.* Denville, N.J.: Dimension Books, 1975. 237p.

Symeon the New Theologian, *see* Symeon Neotheologus

William of St. Thierry, *see* Guillaume de Saint-Thierry

Late Medieval, 1201–1500

Bonaventura, Saint, 1221–1274
Franciscan theologian and scholar, born in Italy. Studied and taught at the University of Paris until he became cardinal bishop of Albano.

J-1   *The Mind's Road to God;* tr. by George Boas. (Library of Liberal Arts, 32) New York: Liberal Arts, 1953. 46p.

J-2   *Rooted in Faith: Homilies to a Contemporary World;* tr. and introd. essay by Marigwen Schumacher. Chicago: Franciscan Herald, 1974. xxxii, 133p.

J-3   *Works of Bonaventure: Cardinal, Seraphic Doctor, and Saint;* tr. by José de Vinck. Paterson, N.J.: St. Anthony Guild Pr., 1966. 5 v.

Especially v.1, *On Perfection of Life Addressed to Sisters,* and v.3, *The Six Wings of the Seraph.*

ABOUT BONAVENTURA:

J-4   Bougerol, Jacques Guy. *Introduction to the Works of Bonaventure.* Chicago: Franciscan Herald, 1964. xiv, 240p.

J-5   Gilson, Etienne. *The Philosophy of Saint Bonaventure.* Chicago: Franciscan Herald, 1965. xv, 499p.

Bonaventure, Saint, *see* Bonaventura, Saint

Caterina da Siena, Saint, 1347–1380
Italian Dominican nun who experienced many visions.

J-6   *The Dialogue of the Seraphic Virgin Dictated by Herself While in a State of Ecstasy* . . .; tr. and introd. on the study of mysticism by Algar Thorold. London: Kegan, Trench, Trübner, 1896. vii, 360p.

ABOUT CATERINA:

J-7   Giordani, Igino. *Saint Catherine of Siena.* Boston: St. Paul Editions, 1975. 258p.

J-8   Raymundus da Vineis. *The Life of St. Catherine of Siena,* by Blessed Raymond of Capua. London: Harvill Pr., 1960. 384p.

Catherine of Siena, *see* Caterina da Siena

THE CLOUD OF UNKNOWING
    An important mystical treatise by an unknown author of 14th-century England.

J-9   *The Cloud of Unknowing;* introd. commentary and tr. by Ira Progoff. New York: Julian, 1957. 243p.

J-10   *The Cloud of Unknowing and the Book of Privy Counseling;* ed. and introd. by William Johnston. Garden City, N.Y.: Doubleday, 1973. 195p.

ABOUT THE CLOUD OF UNKNOWING:

J-11   Johnston, William. *The Mysticism of the Cloud of Unknowing: A Modern Interpretation;* foreword by Thomas Merton, 2d ed. (Religious Experience Series, v.8) St. Meinrad, Ind.: Abbey Pr., 1975. xviii, 285p.

J-12   Nieva, Constantino Sarmiento. *This Transcending God: The Teaching of the Author of the Cloud of Unknowing.* London: Mitre Pr., 1970. 298p.

Cusanus, Nicholas, *see* Nicolaus Cusanus

Dante, *see* Dante Alighieri

DANTE ALIGHIERI, 1265–1321
    The famous Italian poet.

J-13   *The Divine Comedy;* ed. by Edmund G. Gardner. New York: Dutton, 1961. 451p.

J-14   *Vita Nuova;* tr. by Mark Musa. Bloomington: Indiana Univ. Pr., 1973. xiv, 210p.

ABOUT DANTE:

J-15   Dunbar, Helen Flanders. *Symbolism in Medieval Thought and Its*

Consummation in the Divine Comedy. New Haven: Yale Univ. Pr., 1929. xvii, 563p.

J-16 Gardner, Edmund Garratt. *Dante and the Mystics.* New York: Dutton, 1913. xv, 357p.

ECKHART, meister, 1260–1327
An influential Dominican monk, philosopher, and teacher. Sometimes called the founder of German mysticism.

J-17 *Meister Eckhart: An Introduction to the Study of His Works, with an Anthology of His Sermons,* sel., annot., and tr. by James M. Clark. London: Nelson, 1957. 267p.

J-18 *Meister Eckhart, a Modern Translation;* tr. by Raymond Bernard Blakney. New York: Harper, 1957. 333p.

ABOUT ECKHART:

J-19 Ancelet-Hustache, Jeanne. *Master Eckhart and the Rhineland Mystics.* (Men of Wisdom, 4) New York: Harper, 1957. 190p.

FRANCESCO D'ASSISI, Saint, 1182–1226
A friar who lived in poverty and was noted for his love of nature. Founder of the Franciscan order.

J-20 *The Words of Saint Francis: An Anthology;* comp. and arr. by James Meyer. Chicago: Franciscan Herald, 1966. viii, 359p.

J-21 *The Writings;* tr. by Benen Fahy, introd. and notes by Placid Hermann. Chicago: Franciscan Herald, 1964. 200p.

ABOUT FRANCESCO:

J-22 Armstrong, Edward Allworthy. *Saint Francis: Nature Mystic.* (Hermeneutics Studies in the History of Religions, v.2) Berkeley: Univ. of California Pr., 1963. 270p.

J-23 Cunningham, Lawrence, ed. *Brother Francis: An Anthology of Writings by and about Saint Francis of Assisi.* New York: Harper, 1972. xxii, 201p.

J-24 Smith, John Holland. *Francis of Assisi.* New York: Scribner, 1972. 210p.

Francis of Assisi, *see* Francesco d'Assisi

GERTRUDE, Saint, surnamed the Great, 1256–1302
A Benedictine abbess.

J-25 *The Exercises of Saint Gertrude;* introd., commentary, and tr. by a Benedictine Nun of Regina Laudis. Westminster, Md.: Newman, 1956. 191p.

J-26 *The Life and Revelations of Saint Gertrude. . . .* Westminster, Md.: Newman, 1949. xiv, 570p.

Gregory Palamas, *see* Palamas, Gregorius

HILTON, WALTER, d. 1396
A canon of Thurgarton in Nottinghamshire. Widely read in the 15th century.
J-27   *The Goad of Love: An Unpublished Translation by Walter Hilton of the Stimulus Amoris Formerly Attributed to St. Bonaventure;* ed. from manuscripts by Clare Kirchberger. (Classics of the Contemplative Life) London: Faber, 1952. 223p.
J-28   *The Ladder of Perfection;* tr. and introd. by Leo Sherley-Price. Harmondsworth, England: Penguin, 1957. xxii, 256p.
ABOUT HILTON:
J-29   Milosh, Joseph E. *The Scale of Perfection and the English Mystical Tradition.* Madison: Univ. of Wisconsin Pr., 1966. vii, 216p.

IMITATIO CHRISTI. English.
A devotional classic of the 14th or 15th century whose authorship has been ascribed to both Gerard Groote and Thomas à Kempis.
J-30   *The Imitation of Christ;* ed. and introd. by Harold C. Gardiner. Garden City, N.Y.: Hanover House, 1955. 236p.

Imitation of Christ, *see* Imitatio Christi

JAN VAN RUYSBROECK, 1293–1381
A Flemish Augustinian priest and follower of Meister Eckhart.
J-31   *The Adornment of the Spiritual Marriage. The Sparkling Stone. The Book of Supreme Truth;* ed., introd., and notes by Evelyn Underhill. London: Watkins, 1951. xxxii, 259p.
J-32   *The Spiritual Espousals;* tr. and introd. by Eric Colledge. (Classics of the Contemplative Life) New York: Harper, 1953. 195p.
ABOUT JAN VAN RUYSBROECK:
J-33   Mommaers, Paul. *The Land Within: The Process of Possessing and Being Possessed by God According to the Mystic Jan van Ruysbroeck.* Chicago: Franciscan Herald, 1975. vii, 143p.
J-34   Wautier d'Aygalliers, Alfred. *Ruysbroeck the Admirable.* New York: Dutton, 1925. xliii, 326p.

Joannes Tauler, *see* Tauler, Johannes

John Tauler, *see* Tauler, Johannes

Julian of Norwich, *see* Juliana

JULIANA, anchoret, 1343–1443
Religious recluse attached to the church of Saint Julian near Norwich.

J-35 *The Revelations of Divine Love;* tr. by James Walsh. New York: Harper, 1961. xix, 210p.

J-36 *Shewing of God's Love;* ed. by Anna Marie Reynolds (Spiritual Masters) London: Sheed & Ward, 1974. lviii, 99p.

ABOUT JULIANA:

J-37 Molinari, Paul. *Julian of Norwich: The Teaching of a Fourteenth-Century Mystic.* London: Longmans, 1958. 214p.

KEMPE, MARGERY (Burnham), b. c.1373
An Englishwoman who dictated the story of her spiritual journey.

J-38 *The Book of Margery Kempe, Fourteen Hundred and Thirty-Six.* Modern version by W. Butler-Bowdon. New York: Devin-Adair, 1944. xxvi, 243p.

ABOUT KEMPE:

J-39 Cholmeley, Katherine. *Margery Kempe, Genius and Mystic.* London: Longmans, 1947. xiii, 118p.

J-40 Thornton, Martin. *Margery Kempe: An Example in the English Pastoral Tradition.* London: Society for Promoting Christian Knowledge, 1960. 120p.

LANGLAND, WILLIAM, c.1330–c.1400
English poet.

J-41 *Visions from Piers Plowman;* tr. into modern English by Nevill Coghill. London: Oxford Univ. Pr., 1950. 143p.

ABOUT LANGLAND:

J-42 Hort, Greta. *Piers Plowman and Contemporary Religious Thought.* New York: Macmillan, 1938. 170p.

LULL, RAMÓN, c.1235–1315
A Catalan who experienced visions and became a philosopher, poet, and missionary.

J-43 *The Art of Contemplation;* tr. and introd. essay by E. Allison Peers. New York: Macmillan, 1925. 116p.

ABOUT LULL:

J-44 Peers, Edgar Allison. *Fool of Love: The Life of Ramon Lull.* London: SCM Pr., 1946. 127p.

Lully, Raymond, *see* Lull, Ramón

Master Eckhart, *see* Eckhart, meister

MECHTHILD OF MAGDEBURG, c.1212–c.1282
Dominican nun who joined the Cistercian convent at Helfde.

J-45 *The Revelations of Mechthild of Magdeburg or, the Flowing Light of the Godhead;* tr. and introd. by Lucy Menzies. London: Longmans, 1953. xxxvii, 263p.

Meister Eckhart, *see* Eckhart, meister

Nicholas of Cusa, *see* Nicolaus Cusanus

NICOLAUS CUSANUS, 1401–1464
A German churchman and philosopher who was made a cardinal and tried to institute reforms.

J-46 *Of Learned Ignorance;* tr. by Germain Heron, introd. by D. J. B. Hawkins. (Rare Masterpieces of Philosophy and Literature) New Haven: Yale Univ. Pr., 1954. xxviii, 174p.

J-47 *The Vision of God;* tr. by Emma G. Salter, introd. by Evelyn Underhill. New York: Ungar, 1960. xxx, 130p.

ABOUT NICOLAUS:

J-48 Bett, Henry. *Nicholas of Cusa.* (Great Medieval Churchmen) London: Methuen, 1932. x, 210p.

PALAMAS, GREGORIUS, Archbishop of Thessalonica, c.1296–c.1359
A Byzantine monk and spiritual leader who incorporated Eastern monastic spirituality into a comprehensive theological vision.

ABOUT PALAMAS:

J-49 Meyendorff, Jean. *A Study of Gregory Palamas.* London: Faith Pr., 1964. 241p.

ROLLE, RICHARD, of Hampole, c.1290–1349
An Englishman who became a hermit at the age of nineteen.

J-50 *English Writings of Richard Rolle, Hermit of Hampole;* ed. by Hope Emily Allen. Oxford: Clarendon Pr., 1931. lxiv, 180p.

J-51 *The Fire of Love;* ed. and introd. by Clifton Wolters. Baltimore: Penguin, 1972. 192p.

ABOUT ROLLE:

J-52   Comper, Frances Margaret Mary. *The Life of Richard Rolle, Together with an Edition of His English Lyrics.* New York: Dutton, 1929. xx, 340p.

J-53   Hodgson, Geraldine Emma. *The Sanity of Mysticism: A Study of Richard Rolle.* London: Faith Pr., 1926. 227p.

Ruysbroeck, Jan van, *see* Jan van Ruysbroeck

Suso, Heinrich, c.1300–1366
    Dominican disciple of Meister Eckhart, noted for the lyrical poetic quality of his writing.

J-54   *The Exemplar: Life and Writings of Blessed Henry Suso;* tr. by Ann Edward, critical introd. and explanatory notes by Nicholas Heller. Dubuque, Iowa: Priory Pr., 1962. liii, 234p.

J-55   *Little Book of Eternal Wisdom and Little Book of Truth.* (Classics of the Contemplative Life) New York: Harper, 1953. 212p.

ABOUT SUSO:

J-56   Clark, James Midgley. *The Great German Mystics: Eckhart, Tauler, and Suso.* Oxford: Blackwell, 1949. vii, 121p.

Suso, Henry, *see* Suso, Heinrich

Suss, Henry, *see* Suso, Heinrich

Tauler, Johannes, 1300–1361
    A popular preacher of the Friends of God movement and Dominican disciple of Meister Eckhart.

J-57   *Spiritual Conferences;* tr. and ed. by Eric Colledge and Sister M. Jane. (Cross and Crown Series of Spirituality, no.20) St. Louis: Herder, 1961. 283p.

J-58   Spurious and Doubtful Works:
The Book of the Poor in Spirit, by a Friend of God: A Guide to Rhineland Mysticism; ed., tr., and introd. by C. F. Kelley. New York: Harper, 1954. xv, 288p.

ABOUT TAULER:

J-59   Clark, James Midgley. *The Great German Mystics: Eckhart, Tauler, and Suso.* Oxford: Blackwell, 1949. vii, 121p.

Tauler, John, *see* Tauler, Johannes

Theologia Deutsch
    An anonymous mystical treatise of the second half of the 14th century that influenced many, including Martin Luther. May have been written by a priest of the Teutonic order in Frankfurt.

J-60 *Theologia Germanica: The Way to a Sinless Life;* ed. by Thomas S. Kepler. (World Devotional Classics) Cleveland: World, 1952. 192p.

Reformation and Post-Reformation, 1501–1700

ANDREWES, LANCELOT, 1555–1626
Anglican bishop of Chichester, Ely, and Winchester.

K-1 *The Private Devotions of Lancelot Andrewes;* ed. by Hugh Martin. (Treasury of Christian Books) London: SCM Pr., 1957. xii, 146p.

K-2 *Sermons;* sel., ed., and introd. by G. M. Story. Oxford: Clarendon Pr., 1967. lii, 295p.

ABOUT ANDREWES:

K-3 Reidy, Maurice Francis. *Bishop Lancelot Andrewes, Jacobean Court Preacher: A Study in Early 17th Century Religious Thought.* (Jesuit Studies) Chicago: Loyola Univ. Pr., 1955, xiii, 237p.

Angelus Silesius, *see* Scheffler, Johann

BAKER, AUGUSTINE, 1575–1641
An English Benedictine monk.

K-4 *Holy Wisdom, or Directions for the Prayer of Contemplation.* New York: Benziger, 1890. xx, 667p.

ABOUT BAKER:

K-5 Low, Anthony. *Augustine Baker.* (Twayne English Authors Series, 104) New York: Twayne, 1970. 170p.

BAXTER, RICHARD, 1615–1691
A Puritan divine.

K-6 *The Saints' Everlasting Rest;* introd. by John T. Wilkinson. Westwood, N.J.: Revell, 1962. x, 187p.

ABOUT BAXTER:

K-7 Nuttall, Geoffrey F. *Richard Baxter.* London: Nelson, 1965. lx, 142p.

Boehme, Jacob, *see* Böhme, Jakob

BÖHME, JAKOB, 1575–1624
A German peasant from the Lutheran tradition, whose mystical doctrine, a combination of theology, metaphysics, and practical Christianity, was influential in Europe.

K-8 *Aurora;* tr. by John Sparrow. Rev. ed. London: J. M. Watkins, 1960. 723p.

K-9 *Signature of All Things, and Other Writings;* introd. by Clifford Bax. London: James Clarke, 1969. xii, 295p.

K-10 *Six Theosophic Points, and Other Writings;* introd. essay, "Unground and Freedom," by Nicholas Berdyaev; tr. by John Rolleston Earle. Ann Arbor: Univ. of Michigan Pr., 1958. xii, 208p.

ABOUT BÖHME:

K-11 Brinton, Howard Haines. *The Mystic Will, Based on a Study of the Philosophy of Jacob Boehme.* New York: Macmillan, 1930. xiii, 269p.

K-12 Hartmann, Franz. *The Life and Doctrines of Jacob Boehme, the God-taught Philosopher.* New York: Macoy, 1929. 336p.

CRASHAW, RICHARD, c.1613–1649
English Roman Catholic poet.

K-13 *The Religious Poems of Richard Crashaw;* introd. study by R. A. Eric Shepherd. (The Catholic Library, 10) St. Louis: Herder, 1914. viii, 136p.

ABOUT CRASHAW:

K-14 Williams, George Walton. *Image and Symbol in the Sacred Poetry of Richard Crashaw.* 2d ed. Columbia: Univ. of South Carolina Pr., 1967. 151p.

DONNE, JOHN, 1573–1631
A well-known English poet who was born Roman Catholic and in mid-life took Anglican orders.

K-15 *Devotions upon Emergent Occasions; Together with Death's Duel.* Ann Arbor: Univ. of Michigan Pr., 1959. li, 188p.

K-16 *Prayers of John Donne;* sel. and ed. from earliest sources with essay on Donne's idea of prayer by Herbert H. Umbach. New Haven: College and University Pr., 1951. 109p.

ABOUT DONNE:

K-17 Husain, Itrat. *The Dogmatic and Mystical Theology of John Donne.* New York: Macmillan, 1938. xv, 149p.

Fox, GEORGE, 1624–1691
Son of an English weaver and founder of the Society of Friends (Quakers).

K-18 *Journal;* ed., introd., and notes by Rufus M. Jones, essay on the influence of the Journal by Henry J. Cadbury. New York: Capricorn, 1963. 578p.

ABOUT FOX:

K-19 Jones, Rufus Matthew. *George Fox, Seeker and Friend.* New York: Harper, 1930. 221p.

K-20 Wildes, Harry Emerson. *The Voice of the Lord.* Philadelphia: Univ. of Pennsylvania Pr., 1965. 473p.

Francis de Sales, *see* François de Sales

FRANÇOIS DE SALES, Saint, 1567–1622
Roman Catholic priest who became bishop of Geneva and founder of several religious orders.

K-21 *Introduction to the Devout Life.* New York: Harper, 1950. x, 261p.

ABOUT FRANÇOIS DE SALES:

K-22 Palmer, Christopher Harold. *The Prince Bishop: A Life of St. Francis de Sales.* Ilfracombe, England: Stockwell, 1974. 204p.

K-23 Rivet, Mary Majella. *The Influence of the Spanish Mystics on the Work of St. Francis de Sales.* Washington: Catholic Univ. of America Pr., 1941. xii, 113p.

HERBERT, GEORGE, 1593–1633
English religious poet and clergyman.

K-24 *Poems of George Herbert.* 2d ed. (World's Classics Series, no. 109) London: Oxford Univ. Pr., 1961. xxi, 258p.

ABOUT HERBERT:

K-25 Summers, Joseph Holmes. *George Herbert: His Religion and Art.* Cambridge: Harvard Univ. Pr., 1968. 246p.

HERMAN, NICOLAS, 1611–1691
French soldier and domestic servant who became lay brother of Discalced Carmelites in Paris. Better known as Brother Lawrence.

K-26 *The Practice of the Presence of God.* (Inspirational Classics Series) Old Tappan, N.J.: Revell, 1958. 64p.

Ignacio de Loyola, *see* Loyola, Ignacio de

Ignatius of Loyola, *see* Loyola, Ignacio de

John of the Cross, *see* Juan de la Cruz

JUAN DE LA CRUZ, Saint, 1542–1591
　　Influential Spanish Carmelite friar and ascetic and friend of Teresa of Avila. Wrote some of the world's most popular and well-known mystical works.

K-27　*Ascent of Mount Carmel;* tr., ed., and general introd. by E. Allison Peers. 3d rev. ed. Garden City, N.Y.: Doubleday, 1958. lxxxiv, 386p.

K-28　*Collected Works;* tr. by Kieran Kavanaugh and Otilio Rodriguez. Garden City, N.Y.: Doubleday, 1964. 740p.

K-29　*Dark Night of the Soul;* tr. and ed. by E. Allison Peers. 3d rev. ed. Garden City, N.Y.: Doubleday, 1959. 198p.

K-30　*Living Flame of Love;* tr., ed. and introd. by E. Allison Peers. Garden City, N.Y.: Doubleday, 1962. 272p.

K-31　*Poems of Saint John of the Cross;* Spanish text with tr. by Roy Campbell. New York: Pantheon, 1951. 90p.

ABOUT JUAN DE LA CRUZ:

K-32　Brenan, Gerald. *Saint John of the Cross: His Life and Poetry.* Cambridge: Cambridge Univ. Pr., 1975. xii, 232p.

K-33　Dicken, E. W. Trueman. *The Crucible of Love: A Study on the Mysticism of St. Teresa of Jesus and St. John of the Cross.* New York: Sheed & Ward, 1963. xv, 548p.

K-34　Gicovate, Bernardo. *San Juan de la Cruz.* (Twayne World Authors Series, 141) New York: Twayne, 1971. 153p.

Lawrence, Brother, *see* Herman, Nicolas

LOYOLA, IGNACIO DE, Saint, 1491–1556
　　Spanish soldier of noble descent who was converted to Catholicism and founded the Society of Jesus (Jesuits).

K-35　*Autobiography with Related Documents;* ed., introd., and notes by John C. Olin, tr. by J. O'Callaghan. New York: Harper, 1974. vii, 112p.

K-36　*The Spiritual Exercises of St. Ignatius;* tr. by Anthony Mottola, introd. by Robert J. Gleason. Garden City, N.Y.: Image Books, 1964. 200p.

ABOUT LOYOLA:

K-37　Egan, Harvey. *The Spiritual Exercises and the Ignatian Mystical*

Horizon. (Study Aids on Jesuit Topics, Series 4, no.5) St. Louis: Institute of Jesuit Studies, 1976. 178p.

K-38 Rahner, Hugo. *The Spirituality of St. Ignatius Loyola: An Account of Its Historical Development.* Chicago: Loyola Univ. Pr., 1953. xvii, 142p.

Loyola, Ignatius, *see* Loyola, Ignacio de

MILTON, JOHN, 1608–1674
English poet.

K-39 *Paradise Lost and Selected Poetry and Prose;* ed. and introd. by Northrop Frye. New York: Holt, 1951. 601p.

ABOUT MILTON:

K-40 Bailey, Margaret Lewis. *Milton and Jakob Boehme: A Study of German Mysticism in 17th-Century England.* (Germanic Literature and Culture) London: Oxford Univ. Pr., 1914. vii, 200p.

K-41 Crump, Galbraith Miller. *The Mystical Design of Paradise Lost.* Lewisburg, Pa.: Bucknell Univ. Pr., 1975. 194p.

PASCAL, BLAISE, 1623–1662
French scientist and religious philosopher.

K-42 *Pensées;* tr. and introd. by Martin Turnell. New York: Harper, 1962. 447p.

ABOUT PASCAL:

K-43 Fletcher, Frank Thomas Herbert. *Pascal and the Mystical Tradition.* (Modern Language Studies) New York: Philosophical Library, 1954. vii, 156p.

K-44 MacKenzie, Charles S. *Pascal's Anguish and Joy.* New York: Philosophical Library, 1973. x, 274p.

K-45 Miel, Jan. *Pascal and Theology.* Baltimore: Johns Hopkins Pr., 1969. xv, 216p.

SCHEFFLER, JOHANN, 1624–1677
A German poet ·converted to Catholicism. Wrote under pseudonym of Angelus Silesius.

K-46 *The Book of Angelus Silesius, with Observations by the Ancient Zen Masters;* tr., drawn, and handwritten by Frederick Franck. New York: Vintage, 1976. 145p.

TERESA, Saint, 1515–1582
Spanish nun who founded the Discalced (reformed) Order of Carmelites. With help of her friend, Juan de la Cruz, established thirty-two monasteries. A popular mystical writer.

K-47 *Collected Works of St. Teresa of Avila;* tr. by Kieran Kavanaugh and Otilio Rodriguez. Washington: Institute of Carmelite Studies, 1976. v. 1, 406p.

K-48 *The Interior Castle;* tr. and ed. by E. Allison Peers. Garden City, N.Y.: Doubleday, 1961. 235p.

K-49 *The Life of Teresa of Avila . . . Written by Herself;* tr. by David Lewis, introd. by David Knowles. Westminster, Md.: Newman, 1962. 432p.

K-50 *The Way of Perfection;* tr. and ed. by E. Allison Peers. Garden City, N.Y.: Doubleday, 1964. 280p.

ABOUT TERESA:

K-51 Dicken, E. W. Trueman. *The Crucible of Love: A Study on the Mysticism of St. Teresa of Jesus and St. John of the Cross.* New York: Sheed & Ward, 1963. v, 548p.

K-52 Hatzfeld, Helmut Anthony. *Santa Teresa de Avila.* (Twayne World Authors Series, 79) New York: Twayne, 1969. 200p.

K-53 Thomas, Father, ed. *St. Teresa of Avila;* ed. by Father Thomas and Father Gabriel. Westminster, Md.: Newman, 1963. 249p.

Teresa de Avila, *see* Teresa, Saint

Teresa of Avila, *see* Teresa, Saint

TRAHERNE, THOMAS, 1637–1674
English writer of religious works.

K-54 *Centuries, Poems and Thanksgivings;* ed. by H. M. Margoliouth. London: Oxford Univ. Pr., 1958. 2 v.

ABOUT TRAHERNE:

K-55 Clements, A. L. *The Mystical Poetry of Thomas Traherne.* Cambridge, Mass.: Harvard Univ. Pr., 1969. x, 232p.

K-56 Sherrington, Alison J. *Mystical Symbolism in the Poetry of Thomas Traherne.* St. Lucia, Australia: Univ. of Queensland Pr., 1970. viii, 136p.

VAUGHAN, HENRY, 1622–1695
English religious poet.

K-57 *Complete Poetry*; ed., introd., notes, and variants by French Fogle. New York: New York Univ. Pr., 1965. 541p.

ABOUT VAUGHAN:

K-58 Durr, R. A. *On the Mystical Poetry of Henry Vaughan.* Cambridge, Mass.: Harvard Univ. Pr., 1962. xxi, 178p.

Modern, 1701–1900

BLAKE, WILLIAM, 1757–1827
English artist and poet, noted for his mystical symbolism.

L-1 *Complete Writings, with Variant Readings;* ed. by Geoffrey Keynes. London: Oxford Univ. Pr., 1966. xv, 944p.

ABOUT BLAKE:

L-2 Altizer, Thomas J. *New Apocalypse: The Radical Christian Vision of William Blake.* East Lansing: Michigan State Univ. Pr., 1967. xxi, 226p.

L-3 Berger, Pierre. *William Blake: Poet and Mystic.* New York: Dutton, 1915. xii, 420p.

L-4 Korteling, Jacomina. *Mysticism in Blake and Wordsworth.* Amsterdam: H. J. Paris, 1928. 174p.

L-5 White, Helen Constance. *The Mysticism of William Blake.* (University of Wisconsin Studies in Language and Literature, no.23) Madison: Univ. of Wisconsin Pr., 1927.

BROWNING, ROBERT, 1812–1889
English poet.

L-6 *Paracelsus.* London: Dent, 1904. 155p.

L-7 *The Ring and the Book;* introd. by Wylie Sypher. New York: Norton, 1961. 477p.

ABOUT BROWNING:

L-8 Jones, Rufus Matthew. *Mysticism in Robert Browning.* New York: Macmillan, 1924. 28p.

CAUSSADE, JEAN PIERRE DE, d. 1751
French Jesuit priest and teacher, known for his spiritual writings.

L-9 *Abandonment to Divine Providence;* tr. and introd. by John Beevers. Garden City, N.Y.: Doubleday, 1975. 119p.

L-10 *On Prayer;* introd. by John Chapman. Springfield, Ill.: Templegate, 1960. xxxvii, 273p.

HOPKINS, GERARD MANLEY, 1844–1889
English poet and convert to Roman Catholicism who became a Jesuit.

L-11 *A Hopkins Reader;* sel. and introd. by John Pick. London: Oxford Univ. Pr., 1953. 317p.

ABOUT HOPKINS:

L-12 Downes, David Anthony. *Gerard Manley Hopkins: A Study of His Ignatian Spirit.* New York: Twayne, 1959. 195p.

LAW, WILLIAM, 1686–1761
  Influential English clergyman.

L-13 *Selected Mystical Writings of William Law;* ed., notes, and twenty-four studies in the mystical theology of William Law and Jacob Boehme by Stephen Hobhouse. London: C. W. Daniel, 1938. xvi, 395p.

L-14 *A Serious Call to a Devout and Holy Life;* introd. by J. V. Moldenhawer. Philadelphia: Westminster, 1948. xxv, 353p.

L-15 *The Spirit of Prayer, and The Spirit of Love;* ed. and introd. by Sidney Spencer. Cambridge: James Clarke, 1969. 310p.

ABOUT LAW:

L-16 Hobhouse, Stephen Henry, ed. *William Law and Eighteenth-Century Quakerism.* London: Allen & Unwin, 1927. 342p.

L-17 Walker, Arthur Keith. *William Law: His Life and Thought.* London: Society for Promoting Christian Knowledge, 1973. xiii, 274p.

SWEDENBORG, EMANUEL, 1688–1772
  Swedish theologian, philosopher, and scientist whose followers founded a sect called the Church of the New Jerusalem.

L-18 *The True Christian Religion, Containing the Universal Theology of the New Church;* tr. by Frank C. Bayley, introd. by Helen Keller. New York: Dutton, 1933. xxxii, 928p.

ABOUT SWEDENBORG:

L-19 Spalding, John Howard. *Introduction to Swedenborg's Religious Thought.* New York: Swedenborg Pub. Assn., 1956. 235p.

L-20 Toksvig, Signe. *Emanuel Swedenborg, Scientist and Mystic.* New Haven, Conn.: Yale Univ. Pr., 1948. 389p.

L-21 Van Dusen, Wilson. *The Presence of Other Worlds: The Psychological/Spiritual Findings of Emanuel Swedenborg.* New York: Harper, 1974. xv, 240p.

THÉRÈSE, Saint, 1873–1897
  A French Carmelite nun, sometimes called the Little Flower of Jesus.

L-22 *Story of a Soul: The Autobiography of St. Thérèse of Lisieux;* tr. by John Clarke. Washington: Institute of Carmelite Studies, 1975. xviii, 288p.

ABOUT THÉRÈSE:

L-23 Johnson, Vernon Cecil. *Spiritual Childhood: A Study of Saint Theresa's Teaching.* New York: Sheed & Ward, 1953. 216p.

Thérèse de Lisieux, *see* Thérèse, Saint

Thérèse of Lixieux, *see* Thérèse, Saint

THOMPSON, FRANCIS, 1859–1907
English Catholic poet.

L-24 *Poems;* ed. by Wilfrid Meynell. London: Oxford Univ. Pr., 1960. xi, 367p.

ABOUT THOMPSON:

L-25 Megroz, Rodolphe Louis. *Francis Thompson, the Poet of Earth in Heaven: A Study in Poetic Mysticism.* New York: Scribner, 1927. xiii, 288p.

L-26 Thomson, John. *Francis Thompson, Poet and Mystic.* London: Simpkin, Marshall, 1923. 159p.

THOREAU, HENRY DAVID, 1817–1862
American Transcendentalist essayist, poet, and naturalist.

L-27 *Walden and Other Writings;* ed. and introd. by Brooks Atkinson. New York: Modern Library, 1950. xxiv, 732p.

ABOUT THOREAU:

L-28 Wolf, William J. *Thoreau: Mystic, Prophet, Ecologist.* Philadelphia: United Church, 1974. 223p.

THE WAY OF A PILGRIM
Story of the wanderings and spiritual adventures of an unknown 19th-century Russian pilgrim.

L-29 *The Way of a Pilgrim, and The Pilgrim Continues His Way,* tr. by R. M. French. New York: Seabury, 1965. x, 242p.

WESLEY, JOHN, 1703–1791
English preacher and founder of Methodism.

L-30 *A Plain Account of Christian Perfection.* New ed. London: Epworth, 1968. 116p.

ABOUT WESLEY:

L-31 Haddal, Ingvor. *John Wesley.* Nashville: Abingdon, 1961. 175p.

L-32 Wood, Arthur Skevington. *The Burning Heart: John Wesley, Evangelist.* Grand Rapids, Mich.: Eerdmans, 1967. 302p.

WHITEFIELD, GEORGE, 1714–1770
English evangelistic Methodist preacher.

L-33 *Sermon Outlines: A Choice Collection of 35 Model Sermons;* sel. and ed. by Sheldon B. Quincer. Grand Rapids, Mich.: Eerdmans, 1956. 150p.

ABOUT WHITEFIELD:

L-34 Pollock, John Charles. *George Whitefield and the Great Awakening.* Garden City, N.Y.: Doubleday, 1972. x, 272p.

WOOLMAN, JOHN, 1720–1772
American Quaker known for his opposition to slavery.

L-35 *The Journal and Major Essays;* ed. and introd. by Phillips P. Moulton. (Library of Protestant Thought) London: Oxford Univ. Pr., 1971. xviii, 336p.

ABOUT WOOLMAN:

L-36 Cady, Edwin H. *John Woolman.* New York: Washington Square Pr., 1965. ix, 182p.

L-37 Rosenblatt, Paul. *John Woolman.* (Twayne U. S. Authors Series, 147) New York: Twayne, 1969. 163p.

WORDSWORTH, WILLIAM, 1770–1850
English Romantic poet.

L-38 *Complete Poetical Works;* ed. by A. J. George. (Cambridge Editions Series) Boston: Houghton, 1904. xlii, 937p.

ABOUT WORDSWORTH:

L-39 Korteling, Jacomina. *Mysticism in Blake and Wordsworth.* Amsterdam: H. J. Paris, 1928. 174p.

Contemporary, 1901–

BUBER, MARTIN, 1878–1965
Well-known Jewish theologian and philosopher.

M-1 *Hasidism and Modern Man;* ed. by Maurice Friedman. New York: Horizon, 1958. 256p.

M-2 *I and Thou;* tr. by Ronald Gregor Smith. 2d ed. New York: Scribner, 1970. 185p.

M-3 *Tales of the Hasidim;* tr. by Olga Marx. New York: Schocken, 1970. 2v.

ABOUT BUBER:

M-4 Beek, Martinus Adrianus, and Weiland, J. Sperna. *Martin Buber: Personalist and Prophet*. Westminster, Md.: Newman, 1968. viii, 104p.

M-5 Friedman, Maurice S. *Martin Buber: The Life of Dialogue*. New York: Harper, 1960. viii, 312p.

M-6 Schaeder, Greta. *The Hebrew Humanism of Martin Buber*. Detroit: Wayne State Univ. Pr., 1973. 503p.

DILLARD, ANNIE, 1945–
    American nature writer and winner of Pulitzer Prize.

M-7 *Pilgrim at Tinker Creek*. New York: Harper Magazine Pr., 1974. 271p.

ELIOT, THOMAS STEARNS, 1888–1965
    English poet and critic, born in the United States, who became a convert to Anglicanism.

M-8 *Four Quartets*. New York: Harcourt, 1943. 38p.

M-9 *Murder in the Cathedral*. New York: Harcourt, 1935. 87p.

M-10 *The Wasteland;* ed. by Valerie Eliot. New York: Harcourt, 1971. xxx, 149p.

ABOUT ELIOT:

M-11 Blamires, Harry. *Word Unheard: A Guide through Eliot's* Four Quartets. London: Methuen, 1969. 200p.

M-12 Ishak, Fayek M. *The Mystical Philosophy of T. S. Eliot*. New Haven, Conn.: College & University Pr., 1970. 223p.

M-13 Smidt, Kristian. *Poetry and Belief in the Work of T. S. Eliot*. Rev. ed. New York: Humanities, 1961. xiii, 258p.

HAMMARSKJÖLD, DAG, 1905–1961
    Swedish statesman and secretary general of the United Nations.

M-14 *Markings;* tr. by Leif Sjöberg and W. H. Auden, foreword by W. H. Auden. New York: Knopf, 1964. xxiii, 221p.

ABOUT HAMMARSKJÖLD:

M-15 Van Dusen, Henry Pitney. *Dag Hammarskjöld: The Statesman and His Faith*. New York: Harper, 1967. xv, 240p.

HÜGEL, FRIEDRICH VON, 1852–1925
    English Catholic philosopher and teacher.

M-16 *The Mystical Element of Religion*. London: Dent, 1908. 2v.

ABOUT HÜGEL:

M-17 Whelan, Joseph P. *The Spirituality of Friedrich von Hügel*. New York: Newman, 1972, ©1971. 320p.

HUXLEY, ALDOUS LEONARD, 1894–1963
English-born novelist and essayist.

M-18 *After Many a Summer Dies the Swan.* New York: Harper, 1965. 246p.

M-19 *Island.* New York: Harper, 1962. 335p.

M-20 *Time Must Have a Stop.* New York: Harper, 1965. 282p. *See also* D-7 and G-10.

ABOUT HUXLEY:

M-21 Birnbaum, Milton. *Aldous Huxley's Quest for Values.* Knoxville: Univ. of Tennessee Pr., 1971. x, 230p.

M-22 Holmes, Charles M. *Aldous Huxley and the Way to Reality.* Bloomington: Indiana Univ. Pr., 1970. xiii, 238p.

M-23 Savage, Derek S. *Mysticism and Aldous Huxley.* (Outcast Series of Chapbooks, no. 10) Yonkers, N.Y.: O. Baradinsky, 1947. 23p.

KELLY, THOMAS RAYMOND, 1893–1941
Quaker professor whose life was changed by a profound mystical experience.

M-24 *The Reality of the Spiritual World.* (Pendle Hill Pamphlet, 21) Wallingford, Pa.: Pendle Hill, 1942. 62p.

M-25 *A Testament of Devotion;* with a biographical memoir by Douglas V. Steere. New York: Harper, 1941. 124p.

ABOUT KELLY:

M-26 Kelly, Richard M. *Thomas Kelly: A Biography.* New York: Harper, 1966. 125p.

MERTON, THOMAS, 1915–1968
Roman Catholic convert who became a Trappist monk and world-famous author.

M-27 *The Climate of Monastic Prayer;* foreword by Douglas V. Steere. (Cistercian Studies Series, 1) Washington: Cistercian Publications, 1969. 154p.

M-28 *Conjectures of a Guilty Bystander.* Garden City, N.Y.: Doubleday, 1968. 360p.

M-29 *Contemplation in a World of Action;* introd. by Jean Leclercq. Garden City, N.Y.: Doubleday, 1971. xxii, 384p.

M-30 *Mystics and Zen Masters.* New York: Farrar, 1967. x, 303p.

M-31 *New Seeds of Contemplation.* Norfolk, Conn.: New Directions, 1962. 297p.

M-32 *No Man Is an Island.* New York: Harcourt, 1955. 264p.

M-33 *The Sign of Jonas.* New York: Harcourt, 1953. 362p.

M-34 *The Silent Life.* New York: Farrar, 1957. 178p.

M-35 *Thoughts in Solitude.* New York: Farrar, 1958. 120p.

M-36 *Zen and the Birds of Appetite.* Norfolk, Conn.: New Directions, 1968. ix, 141p.
See also H-13.

ABOUT MERTON:

M-37 Bailey, Raymond. *Thomas Merton on Mysticism.* Garden City, N.Y.: Doubleday, 1975. 239p.

M-38 Hart, Patrick, ed. *Thomas Merton, Monk: A Monastic Tribute.* New York: Sheed & Ward, 1974. x, 230p.

M-39 Higgins, John J. *Merton's Theology of Prayer.* (Cistercian Studies Series, 18) Washington: Cistercian Publications, 1971. xxiv, 159p.

M-40 McInerny, Dennis Q. *Thomas Merton, the Man and His Work.* (Cistercian Studies Series, 27) Washington: Cistercian Publications, 1974. xii, 128p.

M-41 Nouwen, Henri J. *Pray to Live: Thomas Merton, a Contemplative Critic.* Notre Dame, Ind.: Fides, 1972. x, 157p.

Silouan, *see* Siluan

SILUAN, monk, 1866–1938
   Peasant who became monk and influential elder of the Orthodox monastery at Mount Athos.

M-42 *Wisdom from Mount Athos: The Writings of Starets Silouan, 1866–1938;* comp. by Archimandrite Sophrony, tr. by Rosemary Edmonds. Rev. ed. Crestwood, N.Y.: St. Vladimir's Seminary Pr., 1975. 127p.

ABOUT SILUAN:

M-43 Sofronii, Archimandrite. *The Monk of Mount Athos, Staretz Silouan;* tr. by Rosemary Edmonds. Crestwood, N.Y.: St. Vladimir's Seminary Pr., 1973. 124p.

TEILHARD DE CHARDIN, PIERRE, 1881–1955
   French Jesuit, geologist, and paleontologist.

M-44 *The Divine Milieu: An Essay on the Interior Life;* tr. by Norman Denny. New York: Harper, 1960. 160p.

M-45 *The Future of Man;* tr. by Norman Denny. New York: Harper, 1964. 319p.

M-46 *Hymn of the Universe;* tr. by Simon Bartholomew. New York: Harper, 1965. 157p.

M-47 *The Phenomenon of Man;* tr. by Bernard Wall, introd. by Julian Huxley. New York: Harper, 1959. 318p.

ABOUT TEILHARD DE CHARDIN:

M-48 Corbishley, Thomas. *The Spirituality of Teilhard de Chardin.* New York: Paulist, 1971. 126p.

M-49 Lubac, Henri de. *The Religion of Teilhard de Chardin.* Westminster, Md.: Newman, 1967. 380p.

M-50 Lukas, Mary, and Lukas, Ellen. *Teilhard.* Garden City, N.Y.: Doubleday, 1976. 360p.

THURMAN, HOWARD, 1899–
Black American clergyman and professor.

M-51 *Deep Is the Hunger: Meditations for Apostles of Sensitiveness.* New York: Harper, 1951. x, 212p.

M-52 *Disciplines of the Spirit.* New York: Harper, 1963. 127p.

M-53 *The Inward Journey.* New York: Harper, 1961. 155p.

M-54 *Meditations of the Heart.* New York: Harper, 1953. 216p.

ABOUT THURMAN:

M-55 Yates, Elizabeth. *Howard Thurman, Portrait of a Practical Dreamer.* New York: Day, 1964. 249p.

UNDERHILL, EVELYN, 1875–1941
English poet and writer on mysticism.

M-56 *An Anthology of the Love of God, from the Writings of Evelyn Underhill;* ed. by Lumsden Barkway and Lucy Menzies. New York: Morehouse-Barlow, 1953. 220p.

M-57 *The Essentials of Mysticism.* New York: Dutton, 1920. vii, 245p.

M-58 *The Mystic Way.* New York: Dutton, 1913. xiv, 395p.
See also A-49, B-48, C-37, G-12

ABOUT UNDERHILL:

M-59 Armstrong, Christopher. *Evelyn Underhill, 1875–1941: An Introduction to Her Life and Writings.* Grand Rapids, Mich.: Eerdmans, 1976, ©1975. xxiii, 303p.

Von Hügel, Friedrich, *see* Hügel, Friedrich von

WATTS, ALAN WILSON, 1915–1973
English-born philosopher, student, and professor of Eastern and comparative religion, and Episcopalian priest.

M-60 *Behold the Spirit: A Study in the Necessity of Mystical Religion.* New ed. New York: Pantheon, 1971. xxviii, 257p.

M-61 *Beyond Theology.* New York: Pantheon, 1964. xiii, 236p.

M-62 *In My Own Way: An Autobiography, 1951–1965.* New York: Pantheon, 1972. ix, 400p.

ABOUT WATTS:

M-63 Stuart, David, *Alan Watts,* Radnour, Pa.: Chilton, 1976, 250p.

WEIL, SIMONE, 1909–1943
French Jewish philosopher attracted to Roman Catholicism, noted for her social activism.

M-64 *On Science, Necessity, and the Love of God: Essays;* collected, tr., and ed. by Richard Rees. London: Oxford Univ. Pr., 1968. lx, 201p.

M-65 *Seventy Letters;* tr. and arr. by Richard Rees. London: Oxford Univ. Pr., 1965. xiv, 207p.

M-66 *Waiting for God;* tr. by Emma Craufurd; introd. by Leslie Fiedler. New York: Harper, 1973. xi, 227p.

ABOUT WEIL:

M-67 Anderson, David. *Simone Weil.* London: SCM Pr., 1971. 121p.

M-68 Davy, Marie Magdeleine. *The Mysticism of Simone Weil.* London: Rockcliff, 1951. 84p.

M-69 Pètrement, Simone. *Simone Weil: A Life.* New York: Pantheon, 1976. 577p.

M-70 Rees, Richard. *Simone Weil: A Sketch for a Portrait.* Carbondale: Southern Illinois Univ. Pr., 1966. viii, 205p.

Appendix: a guide for Acquisitions librarians

The appendix lists first-purchase recommendations for a basic collection of materials on Western mysticism and for a collection of popular titles on the subject.

Basic Collection

Many of the titles listed are still in print or have been reprinted.

1. THE PHILOSOPHY OF MYSTICISM

A-9 Dupré, L. K. *The Other Dimension: A Search for the Meaning of Religious Attitudes.*

A-11 Eliade, M. *Myths, Dreams and Mysteries.*

A-12 Furse, M. L. *Mysticism: Window on a World View.*

A-17 Happold, F. C. *Religious Faith and Twentieth-Century Man.*

A-18 Harkness, G. *Mysticism: Its Meaning and Message.*

A-20 Herman, E. *The Meaning and Value of Mysticism.*

A-21 Heschel, A. J. *God in Search of Man.*

A-26 James, W. *Varieties of Religious Experience.*

A-29 Jones, R. M. *New Studies in Mystical Religion.*

A-31 Knowles, D. *The Nature of Mysticism.*

A-32 Lossky, V. *The Mystical Theology of the Eastern Church.*

A-35 Nowell, R. *What a Modern Catholic Believes about Mysticism.*

A-40 Scharfstein, B. *Mystical Experience.*

A-43 Spencer, S. *Mysticism in World Religion.*

A-44 Staal, F. *Exploring Mysticism: A Methodological Essay.*

A-46 Stiernotte, A. P., ed. *Mysticism and the Modern Mind.*

A-47   Thornton, M. *English Spirituality: An Outline of Ascetical Theology.*

A-49   Underhill, E. *Mysticism.*

2. THE HISTORY OF MYSTICISM

B-1   Bancroft, A. *Twentieth Century Mystics and Sages.*

B-3   Bolshakoff, S. *Russian Mystics.*

B-5   Bridges, L. H. *American Mysticism.*

B-6   Brinton, H. H. *Friends for 300 Years.*

B-7   Bullett, G. W. *The English Mystics.*

B-8   Butler, E. C. *Western Mysticism.*

B-9   Cheney, S. *Men Who Have Walked with God.*

B-11   Coleman, T. W. *English Mystics of the Fourteenth Century.*

B-16   Graef, H. C. *The Light and the Rainbow.*

B-18   ———. *The Story of Mysticism.*

B-22   Inge, W. R. *Christian Mysticism.*

B-24   Jones, R. M. *The Flowering of Mysticism.*

B-26   ———. *Studies in Mystical Religion.*

B-28   Knowles, D. *The English Mystical Tradition.*

B-29   Knox, R. A. *Enthusiasm.*

B-31   Leclercq, J. *The Love of Learning and the Desire for God.*

B-36   Meyendorff, J. *Saint Gregory Palamas and Orthodox Spirituality.*

B-39   Pepler, C. *The English Religious Heritage.*

B-45   *The Spirituality of Western Christendom,* ed. by E. R. Elder.

B-46   Squire, A. *Asking the Fathers.*

B-47   Stace, W. T. *The Teachings of the Mystics.*

B-48   Underhill, E. *Mystics of the Church.*

B-51   Weiner, H. *9½ Mystics: The Kabbala Today.*

B-52   Wiesel, E. *Souls on Fire.*

3. THE PRACTICE OF MYSTICISM

C-3   Brooke, A. *Doorway to Meditation, in Words and Pictures.*

C-7   Evdokimoff, P. *The Struggle with God.*

C-10   Happold, F. C. *The Journey Inwards.*

C-12   Heschel, A. J. *Man's Quest for God: Studies in Prayer and Symbolism.*

C-13   Hinson, E. G. *A Serious Call to a Contemplative Life Style.*

C-15   Jacobs, L. *Hasidic Prayer.*

C-17   Kelsey, M. *The Other Side of Silence.*

C-19   LeShan, L. *How to Meditate.*

C-21   McNamara, W. *The Human Adventure.*

C-22   Maloney, G. A. *The Breath of the Mystic.*

C-24   Nouwen, H. J. *Reaching Out.*
C-27   Paulsell, W. O. *Taste and See.*
C-28   Pearce, J. *The Crack in the Cosmic Egg.*
C-29   Pennington, B. *Daily We Touch Him.*
C-31   Raguin, Y. *How to Pray Today.*
C-35   Smith, B. *Meditation: The Inward Art.*
C-37   Underhill, E. *Practical Mysticism.*

4. THE EXPERIENCE OF MYSTICISM

D-2   Braden, W. *The Private Sea: LSD and the Search for God.*
D-3   Bucke, R. M. *Cosmic Consciousness.*
D-4   Clark, W. H. *Chemical Ecstasy.*
D-5   Greeley, A. M. *Ecstasy: A Way of Knowing.*
D-10   Johnston, W. *Silent Music.*
D-11   Laski, M. *Ecstasy: A Study of Some Secular and Religious Experiences.*
D-12   LeShan, L. *The Medium, the Mystic, and the Physicist.*
D-13   Leuba, J. H. *The Psychology of Religious Mysticism.*
D-14   Marechal, J. *Studies in the Psychology of the Mystics.*
D-15   Maslow, A. H. *Religions, Values, and Peak-experiences.*
D-18   Naranjo, C., and Ornstein, R. *On the Psychology of Meditation.*
D-19   Ornstein, R. E., ed. *The Nature of Human Consciousness.*
D-21   Pratt, J. B. *The Religious Consciousness.*
D-24   Tart, C. T., ed. *Transpersonal Psychologies.*
D-27   White, J. W., ed. *The Highest State of Consciousness.*

5. ORIENTAL MYSTICISM IN WESTERN CONTEXTS

E-1   Déchanet, J. M. *Christian Yoga.*
E-3   Graham, A. *Contemplative Christianity.*
E-6   Griffiths, B. *Vedanta and Christian Faith.*
E-7   Johnston, W. *Christian Zen.*
E-8   ———. *The Still Point: Reflections on Zen and Christian Mysticism.*
E-9   Lassalle, H. *Zen Meditation for Christians.*
E-11   Raguin, Y. *The Depth of God.*
E-12   Suzuki, D. T. *Mysticism, Christian and Buddhist.*

6. MYSTICAL EXPRESSION IN LITERATURE

F-3   Bremond, H. *Prayer and Poetry.*
F-4   Brockington, A. A. *Mysticism and Poetry on a Basis of Experience.*
F-6   Collins, J. B. *Christian Mysticism in the Elizabethan Age.*

F-8 Durr, R. A. *Poetic Vision and the Psychedelic Experience.*
F-13 Martz, L. L. *The Paradise Within.*
F-14 ———. *Poetry of Meditation.*
F-16 Spurgeon, C. F. E. *Mysticism in English Literature.*
F-21 Wright, L. M. *The Literary Life of the Early Friends, 1650–1725.*

7. MYSTICAL AND CONTEMPLATIVE WRITINGS

Collections

G-1 Colledge, E., ed. *The Mediaeval Mystics of England.*
G-3 *Early Fathers from the Philokalia.*
G-5 Fedotov, G. P., ed. *A Treasury of Russian Spirituality.*
G-8 Happold, F. C. *Mysticism: A Study and an Anthology.*
G-10 Huxley, A. L. *The Perennial Philosophy.*
G-12 Kepler, T. S., ed. *The Fellowship of the Saints.*
G-13 Khariton, comp. *The Art of Prayer: An Orthodox Anthology.*
G-14 Martz, L. L., ed. *The Meditative Poem: An Anthology of Seventeenth-Century Verse.*
G-15 Newman, L. I., ed. *Hasidic Anthology.*
G-16 O'Brien, E. *Varieties of Mystic Experience.*
G-19 Petry, R. C., ed. *Late Mediaeval Mysticism.*
G-23 *Writings from the Philokalia on Prayer of the Heart.*

Ancient, 33–600

ANTONIUS, THE GREAT, Saint
H-1 Athanasius, Saint. *The Life of Saint Anthony.*
AUGUSTINUS, AURELIUS, Saint
H-2 *Basic Writings of Saint Augustine.*
H-5 Butler, E. C. *Western Mysticism: The Teaching of Augustine, Gregory and Bernard on Contemplation and the Contemplative Life.*
CASSIANUS, JOANNES
H-11 Chadwick, O. *John Cassian: A Study in Primitive Monasticism.*
DESERT FATHERS
H-12 Apophthegmata Patrum. *The Sayings of the Desert Fathers.*
EVAGRIUS PONTICUS
H-17 *The Praktikos. Chapters on Prayer.*
ORIGENES
H-28 *Selections from the Commentaries and Homilies of Origen.*
H-30 Daniélou, J. *Origen.*
PACHOMIUS, Saint

FRANCESCO D'ASSISI, Saint
J-20   *The Words of Saint Francis: An Anthology.*
HILTON, WALTER
J-28   *The Ladder of Perfection.*
IMITATIO CHRISTI
J-30   *The Imitation of Christ.*
JAN VAN RUYSBROECK
J-32   *The Spiritual Espousals.*
JULIANA, anchoret
J-36   *Shewing of God's Love.*
ROLLE, RICHARD, of Hampole
J-50   *English Writings of Richard Rolle, Hermit of Hampole.*
SUSO, HEINRICH
J-54   *The Exemplar: Life and Writings of Blessed Henry Suso.*
TAULER, JOHANNES
J-57   *Spiritual Conferences.*

Reformation and Post-Reformation, 1501–1700
ANDREWES, LANCELOT
K-1   *The Private Devotions of Lancelot Andrewes,* ed. by Hugh Martin.
BAKER, AUGUSTINE
K-4   *Holy Wisdom, or Directions for the Prayer of Contemplation.*
BÖHME, JAKOB
K-10   *Six Theosophic Points, and Other Writings.*
DONNE, JOHN
K-15   *Devotions upon Emergent Occasions; Together with Death's Duel.*
FOX, GEORGE
K-18   *Journal;* ed., introd., notes by Rufus M. Jones.
FRANÇOIS DE SALES
K-21   *Introduction to the Devout Life.*
JUAN DE LA CRUZ, Saint
K-28   *Collected Works.*
K-33   Dicken, E. W. T. *The Crucible of Love: A Study on the Mysticism of St. Teresa of Jesus and St. John of the Cross.*
LOYOLA, IGNACIO DE, Saint
K-35   *Autobiography with Related Documents.*
K-36   *The Spiritual Exercises of St. Ignatius.*
MILTON, JOHN
K-39   *Paradise Lost and Selected Poetry and Prose.*
PASCAL, BLAISE
K-42   *Pensées.*

Collection of Popular Titles

Titles recommended are on an introductory and popular level. All are in print and almost all are available in paperback.

A-12 Furse, *Mysticism, Window on a World View.*
A-37 Otto, *Idea of the Holy.*
A-41 Scholem, *Major Trends in Jewish Mysticism.*
 B-3 Bolshakoff, *Russian Mystics.*
C-17 Kelsey, *The Other Side of Silence.*
C-23 Maloney, *Inward Stillness.*
C-29 Pennington, *Daily We Touch Him.*
C-31 Raguin, *Paths to Contemplation.*
C-34 Slade, *Exploration into Contemplative Prayer.*
 D-5 Greeley, *Ecstasy: A Way of Knowing.*
D-18 Naranjo and Ornstein, *On the Psychology of Meditation.*
 E-7 Johnston, *Christian Zen*
 E-8 ———, *The Still Point: Reflections on Zen and Christian Mysticism.*
G-21 Reinhold, *The Soul Afire: Revelations of the Mystics.*
 J-9 *The Cloud of Unknowing.*
J-11 Johnston, *The Mysticism of the Cloud of Unknowing: A Modern Interpretation.*
K-42 Pascal, *Pensées.*
L-27 Thoreau, *Walden and Other Writings.*
M-25 Kelly, *A Testament of Devotion.*
M-27 Merton, *Climate of Monastic Prayer.*
M-31 ———, *New Seeds of Contemplation.*
M-37 Bailey, *Thomas Merton on Mysticism.*

AUTHOR-TITLE INDEX

Titles issued as separate publications are underlined. Titles published within collections are enclosed in quotation marks. Series titles are followed by the word *series*. Numbers cited are item numbers.

Aaronson, Bernard S., D-23
Abandonment to Divine Providence, L-9
Abhishiktananda, *see* LeSaux, Henri
About the Contemplative Life, H-35
"Adam of Dryburgh," B-49
Adornment of the Spiritual Marriage, J-31
Advice to a Pope, I-3
Aelred of Rievaulx, *see* Ethelred, Saint
Aelred of Rievaulx, a Study, I-14
After Many a Summer Dies the Swan, M-18
Agreda, María de, G-20
Alabaster, William, G-14
Alan Watts, M-63
Aldous Huxley and the Way to Reality, M-22
Aldous Huxley's Quest for Values, M-21
Alpert, Richard, D-1
Altered States of Consciousness, D-23
"Altered States of Consciousness," D-27
Altizer, Thomas J., L-2
American Mystical Verse, G-9
American Mysticism, B-5
Ames, Adelbert, Jr., D-19

Among the Mystics, B-13
Anagogic Qualities of Literature, F-1
Anand, B. K., D-23
Ancelet-Hustache, Jeanne, J-19
"Anchoresses' Guide," B-49
Ancient Christian Writers series, H-1, H-19, H-27, I-24
Anderson, David, M-67
Andreach, Robert J., F-2
Andrewes, Lancelot, G-12, K-1–2
Andrews, Charles F., G-12
Angela of Foligno, Saint, G-11
Angeles, Juan de los, G-18, G-20
Angelus Silesius, pseud., *see* Scheffler, Johann
Anselm, Father, K-53
Anselm, Saint, G-11, I-1
Anthology of Mysticism, G-11
Anthology of Seventeenth-Century Verse, G-14
Anthology of the Love of God, M-56
Anthology of Writings by and about Saint Francis of Assisi, J-23
Anthony, Saint, *see* Antonius the Great, Saint
"Antithesis and Argument in the *De Consideratione*," I-7
Antonius the Great, Saint, G-3, H-1

Jesus Prayer, C-33
Joannes Climacus, H-24
John, Saint, G-8, G-23
John Cassian, *see* Cassianus, Joannes
John Cassian, H-11
John Climacus, *see* Joannes Climacus
John of Cronstadt, G-5
John of Ruysbroeck, *see* Jan van
   Ruysbroeck
John of the Cross, *see* Juan de la
   Cruz
John Tauler, *see* Tauler, Johannes
John Wesley, L-31
John Wesley, Evangelist, L-32
John Woolman, L-36–37
Johnson, Pierce, A-27
Johnson, Rayner C., D-8–9
Johnson, Vernon C., L-23
Johnson, William A., A-28
Johnston, William, D-10, E-7–8,
   J-10–11
Jones, E. Stanley, G-12
Jones, Rufus M., A-29, B-24–26,
   G-12, K-18–19, L-8
Jordan, G. Ray, Jr., D-27
*Journal and Major Essays of John
   Woolman,* L-35
Journal of George Fox, K-18
Journey Inwards, C-10
"Joy in This World and Confidence
   in the Next," F-1
Juan de la Cruz, Saint, G-8,
   G-11–12, G-16, G-18, G-20,
   K-27–31
Julian of Norwich, *see* Juliana
Julian of Norwich, J-37
"Julian of Norwich," B-49
Juliana, Anchoret, G-1, G-8,
   G-11–12, G-16, J-35–36
Jung, Carl G., D-19
Justin Martyr, G-12

Kabbalah, B-41
Kadloubovsky, E., G-3, G-13, G-23
Kagawa, Toyohiko, G-12

Kamiya, Joe, D-19, D-23
Kanellakos, Demetri P., D-27
Kaplan, Nathanial, B-27
Kapleau, Philip, D-19
Kasamatsu, Akira, D-19, D-23
"Kasina Exercises: Dharana," D-19
Katsaros, Thomas, B-27
Katz, Joseph, H-38
Kavanaugh, Kieran, K-28, K-47
Keller, Helen, L-18
Kelley, C. F., J-58
Kelly, Richard M., M-26
Kelly, Thomas R., G-12, M-24–25
Kelsey, Morton T., A-30, C-17
Kempe, Margery, G-1, G-7, G-12,
   J-38
Kennan, Elizabeth T., I-7
Kepler, Thomas S., G-12, J-60
Keynes, Geoffrey, L-1
Khariton, G-13
Kiefer, Durand, D-27
Kierkegaard, Søren, G-12
Killam, Keith, D-1
Kilpatrick, F. P., D-19
Kirchberger, Clare, I-28, J-27
Knowles, David, A-31, B-28, B-50,
   K-49
Knox, John, G-12
Knox, Ronald A., B-29
Koppers, Wilhelm, A-34
Korteling, Jacomina, L-4, L-39
Kovalevsky, Pierre, B-30
Kretschmer, Wolfgang, D-23
Krippner, Stanley, D-23, D-27
Krueger, A. P., D-19

"LSD and Mystical Experience,"
   D-27
LSD and the Search for God, D-2
"LSD 'Regulars'," D-1
Ladder of Divine Ascent, H-24
Ladder of Perfection, J-28
Laing, R. D., D-27
Lallemant, Louis, G-11
Land Within, J-33

"Mysticism and Ethics," A-46

"Mysticism and Existentialism,"
A-46

"Mysticism and Modern West
African Writing," F-1

"Mysticism and Mystery," A-50

"Mysticism and Naturalistic
Humanism," A-46

Mysticism and Philosophy, A-45

*Mysticism and Poetry on a Basis of
Experience*, F-4

"Mysticism and Schizophrenia,"
D-27

Mysticism and the Eastern Church,
A-1

"Mysticism and the Limits of
Communication," A-46

"Mysticism and the Modern Mind,"
A-46

Mysticism and Theology, A-48

Mysticism, Christian and Buddhist,
E-12

Mysticism, East and West, E-10

*Mysticism in Blake and
Wordsworth*, L-4, L-39

Mysticism in English Literature,
F-16

Mysticism in Religion, A-25

Mysticism in Robert Browning, L-8

*Mysticism in Seventeenth Century
English Literature*, F-17

Mysticism in the Neo-Romanticists,
F-5

Mysticism in World Religion, A-43

*Mysticism: Its Meaning and
Message*, A-18

Mysticism of Paul the Apostle, H-33

Mysticism of Simone Weil, M-68

*Mysticism of the Cloud of
Unknowing*, J-11

Mysticism of William Blake, L-5

Mysticism, Old and New, A-23

Mysticism, Sacred and Profane, A-54

Mysticism, Science and Revelation,
A-42

*Mysticism: Window on a World
View*, A-12

Mystics and Heretics in Italy . . . ,
B-14

Mystics and Militants, B-12

Mystics and Society, A-14

Mystics and Zen Masters, M-30

Mystics of Our Time, B-17

Mystics of Spain, G-18

Mystics of the Church, B-48

Myth and Reality, A-10

Myth, History and Faith, A-30

Myths, Dreams and Mysteries, A-11

Nambiar, O. K., F-1

Naranjo, Claudio, D-18–19

Natural Depth in Man, D-25

"Natural History of LSD Use," D-1

"Nature in Islamic Thought," A-34

Nature of Human Consciousness, D-19

Nature of Mysticism, A-31

"Nature of Psi Processes," D-19

Need for Contemplation, C-39

Neisser, Ulric, D-19

Neumann, Erich, A-34

New Apocalypse, L-2

New Seeds of Contemplation, M-31

New Studies in Mystical Religion,
A-29

Newman, John Henry, G-12

Newman, Louis I., G-15

Nicephorus the Solitary, G-23

Nicholas of Cusa, *see* Nicolaus
Cusanus

Nicholas of Cusa, J-48

Nicholl, Donald, B-49

Nicholson, D. H. S., G-17

Nicolaus Cusanus, G-8, G-12, G-19,
J-46–47

Niebuhr, Reinhold, G-12

Nieremberg, Juan Eusebio, G-20

Nieva, Constantino S., J-12

Nikam, N. A., A-46

Nilaus of Sinai, Saint, G-3

9½ Mystics, B-51

sUBJECT iNDEX

ACP-0913

3/8/94

BL
625
A1
B68
1978